SWAT

Seize the Accomplishment

by Timothy L. Johnson

Also by Timothy L. Johnson

Race Through the Forest - A Project Management Fable
GUST - The "Tale" Wind of Office Politics

More Praise for SWAT

More Praise for SWAT

"Timothy Johnson's book *SWAT* provides an excellent example of how to apply systems thinking in a business environment. Told from the perspective of a middle manager who had been with a company since it's start-up phase, Johnson uses a police SWAT team leader as the guide who helps the manager resolve a customer service challenge where external consultants have failed. Throughout the book, Johnson weaves in SWAT team examples to illustrate how to apply the various aspects of systems thinking to the process of turning a bad performing customer service team into one that works collaboratively to solve problems and serve the customer. It's an easy read, goes quickly, and keeps the reader engaged. I highly recommend it."

—Jeri Denniston
Chief Marketing Strategist, Haines Centre for Strategic Management

"Timothy Johnson has captured a unique position with organizations and how they improve and change successfully. If we do not consider the systems as a whole in an organization and how they interact, any change we make is likely to be short-lived."

—Martin K. Berndt
Vice President, Continuous Improvement, Teva Brand Pharmaceuticals

"Timothy Johnson's book *SWAT* is a must-read for every aspiring (and practicing) business analyst, process manager, and project manager. It is the best business novel/fable/non-nonfiction business book around (this from someone who lists *The Goal*, *It's Not Luck*, and *Critical Chain* as 3 of the 5 best business books he's read). It is a clear, concise, entertaining, and EFFECTIVE introduction to systems thinking. Thank you, Tim!"

—Mike DeWitt
Chief Operating Officer, Cyberactive Marketing LLC

"What a fantastic way to present what many people believe to be such a confusing subject. Not only did Timothy Johnson hit the marks on the basics of analysis but he also did a great job presenting the implementation of those basics. I would consider this book a recommended read to all my Business Analyst peers! Great Job!"

—Robin Tracy, PMP, CBAP
President, Advanced Solutions Consulting, Inc.

"Timothy Johnson hits another home run with *SWAT*! As someone who has worked with all the intricate processes involved in a call center, the analogy between a SWAT team and a project team to solve a call center's problems is on the mark and easy for everyone to understand and put into action."

—Phil Gerbyshak
Author, SlackerManager.com and *10 Ways to Make it Great*!

"Who doesn't want to be a better thinker? As the detailed drool-over-it stuff of great projects, systems thinking is something everyone in business needs to get on board with—now. Most of us think we understand it, and say we do, for the basics are not that hard to grasp, yet we all mess up because we really don't get it. Timothy Johnson has done us a tremendous favor with *SWAT*, for his book is slim-quick and story-enjoyable reading, and not the dry textbook presentation you'll normally suffer through. Finally, here is a book you can hand to everyone involved with your next project, being sure they will devour it quickly—and then use it forevermore. In fact, once you read it, I'm sure you will think of a bunch of existing systems that need a good swift *SWAT* too."

—Rosa Say, founder of Say Leadership Coaching; Author,
Managing with Aloha

Printed in the U.S.A.
ISBN 978-1-934417-02-7

Acknowledgements

To Lauren and Abby and Shannon – the best "inputs" and "outputs" are often times under my own roof—for your continued support through writers' block and sudden bursts of inspiration.

To Lt. Travis Ouverson (West Des Moines PD) and Sgt. Kent Knopf (Urbandale PD) – for inviting me into your world and allowing me to see the true heart of what makes SWAT work. Your mentoring, encouragement, feedback, support, and inspiration have breathed more life into this book than my imagination ever could.

To Detective Cari McDaniel (Urbandale PD) – for sharing with me so many thoughts about effective negotiation tactics and how they fit in with the big picture.

To Field Training Officer Chris Greenfield (Urbandale PD) and Officer Daniel Jansen (West Des Moines PD) – for the all-night ride-alongs and allowing me to bombard you with a continuous flow of questions about how you do your job.

To Sr. Officer Charles Masterson (West Des Moines PD) – for your continued wisdom and insight. Your sage guidance was the cornerstone for "consistent where critical; variable where valued."

To the remaining members of the SERT team – just for being who you are: brave, heroic, insightful, honest, hardworking, and fun people who do a tough job very well. My respect for your profession has increased exponentially. I appreciate your willingness to let me tag along, to watch, to ask questions … and I appreciate that you always just acted like yourselves when I was with you.

continued on next page

Altoona PD
Sergeant Royal Kerchee
Sergeant. Jary Bowie
Detective Jason Ferguson

Officer Amos Purcell
Officer Mark Harmon
Officer Louis Miner

Clive PD
Detective Matthew Barron

Sergeant Damon Herzog

Johnston PD
Officer Jason Gudenkauf

Officer Matt Stringham

Windsor Heights PD
Captain Dennis McDaniel

Urbandale PD
Chief Ross McCarty
Retired Chief Dave Hamlin
Sergeant Matt Logsdon
Officer Steve Shivers
Officer Matt Gausman
Officer Mike Haydon
Officer Andy Dobbins
Officer Kip Liston

Officer Shawn Popp
Officer Shane Taylor
Officer Chad Underwood
Officer Mark Jorgensen
Officer Ryan Neumann
Officer Andy Morlan
Officer John McElwee
Officer Matt Flattery

West Des Moines PD
Lieutenant. Michael Ficcola
Sergeant Jason Bryan
Officer Brent Kock
Officer Chris Vesey
Officer. William Taylor III
Officer Anthony Giampolo
Officer Kraig Kincaid
Officer Jeremy Kemmer
Officer Nathan Ladwig

Officer Ryan Purdy
Officer Adam Porath
Officer Eric Donielson
Officer Tanya Zaglauer
Lieutenant Monty Doll,
    WDM EMS
Dr. David G. Stilley,
    MD, FACEP
Dr. Philip A. Bear, DO, FACC

To the team at Lexicon – for your dedication to your craft which allows me to sleep at night. I can't thank you all enough for all of the expertise you bring to the table to help me follow my dreams.

To my family – especially my Mom, Brad and Shelley, David and Jane, Don and Saundra, Blake and Sara, Chuck and Ann – for being my continual cheering section.

To Shane Schulte, J. Erik Potter, Donna Scheidt, Jay Boomershine, Liz Strauss, Troy Worman, and Drew McLellan – for your ideas on the editing process and for making this a better product.

To Josh West – for the great author photos, thanks for investing your time and for your friendship

To Mark Yontz – for providing your special editing insights to this book. It's great to have a creative peer who respects the art and craft of writing as much as you do.

To Delaney Kirk – I continue to be amazed and humbled by our friendship. Thank you for always allowing me to be myself.

To Mike Wagner – for your encouragement to "keep creating" which helps motivate me to "seize the accomplishment."

To Adam Cardinal, Jeff Hutton and Buck Sommerkamp – knowing you're a phone call away has been a lifesaver. Your support and friendship means a lot.

To my colleagues, students, friends, and clients – thank you for continuing to provide me with an endless stream of inspiration.

To God, through whom all things are possible.

Introduction

Are you getting things done?

No, I didn't ask if you were busy. We're all busy. I'll go toe-to-toe with you on daily planners and schedules and task lists. It's a no-win competition, since there are so many things competing for our attention and time and energy.

But are you getting things done? Is all of that busyness accomplishing anything?

Name your top five accomplishments of the past year. How long did each take you? Are these accomplishments you are really proud of, or were they just check marks? Would those with whom you are closest agree with your accomplishments?

When I started my company, Carpe Factum, Inc., it was to address one single issue: ACCOMPLISHMENT. I wrote my first book, *Race Through The Forest—A Project Management Fable*, because I saw my clients struggling to implement their accomplishments. I wrote my second book, *GUST—The "Tale" Wind of Office Politics*, because I saw my colleagues fighting with resistance to their accomplishments. But there was something missing ... then it hit me: How do we design our accomplishments? How do we proactively plan out those future significant check marks in our lives and our businesses?

At heart, I am, have always been, and shall always be, a "process guy." I like to dissect EVERYTHING in terms of a process. What comes before what? What actions create what consequences? When can certain inputs be introduced into the system? How many inputs can be transformed into outputs? What are the hand-offs? Are they happening effectively and efficiently? These are the questions that haunt and taunt me. They are the lens through which I see my world. And they are the reason for my success ... as a consultant, as a professor, as a parent ... you name it. But the question that permeates everything, the one that really triggers every fiber in my mind and soul: "What accomplishments need to be created and how do we get there?"

The answer to accomplishing critical outcomes is the system. Not computer systems, but general systems thinking, which has been recognized for decades and has existed since the beginning of time. If you learn to identify the systems around you and unlock their secrets, it can and will lead you to successful accomplishments. We experience systems all around us, and their importance is becoming more evident with each passing moment. This book takes you to the basics of systems, and then shows you how to break down the system into its components, interpret them, manipulate them, and ultimately change them for the better.

Systems thinking is not just a business issue. It applies to our relationships and our daily transactions. Human behavior and communication both anchor their core to systems application. How we work together as people is a system, and the principles learned in this book will help you accomplish better results in your personal and business relationships. What you are holding in your hands is, in essence, a how-to manual to apply systems in your business, your relationships … basically, in your life in order to accomplish the outputs you desire.

As with my other two books, I took a story approach. I'm becoming less enamored with the term "business fable," although it is the label which seems to stick with this genre of writing. I stay with the story format for two reasons: 1) relevance: you can sit and read pages and pages of systems theory for hours and hours until your eyes glaze over, or you can digest this book in less than two hours during an airplane ride or a couple of lunches. As professionals, our time is limited. Given the choice, I'd rather spend my time accomplishing something great than just sitting around reading about it. 2) entertainment—let's face it … we all love a good story. We remember stories. They become part of our collective consciousness. We may not always be able to dissect the themes or the author's motives for a plot, but we love to cheer for heroes and boo at villains. The characters in this book are very real to me. I've lived some of it personally. I've met some of these people during my journey. Many of the characters are composites and conglomerations of those I've met, but that doesn't make them any less real. Trust me, in our cubicles and offices and factories, there are still heroes and villains.

However you use this book is up to you. The desired output for me is that you see your world, you work, and your relationships a bit differently after you've read it. Systems thinking is universal, and it is a powerful tool to those who know how to leverage it effectively.

One small caveat: I take a few playful swipes at Lean and Six Sigma. While these approaches are sound, I've never been a big fan of methodologies. More accurately, I've never been a fan of people who clamp onto any one methodology like it is THE solution and then dogmatically close their minds to other possibilities. You'll find the principles in this book actually mesh well with Six Sigma and Lean principles, as both support systems thinking. All I ask is that you maintain an open mind about all processes … generally the answers always lie somewhere in the cross-hairs.

So let's get started. Are you ready to illuminate your own business landscape? Are you ready for some hard-core results? Are you ready to look past the fluff of a business world where the latest business fads promise solutions to virtually every business problem? Are you ready to seize the accomplishments waiting for you at the other end?

Carpe Factum!
Timothy Johnson
January, 2010

Prologue

"Oft expectation fails, and oft where most it promises."

-William Shakespeare

"Hi Toby, this is Sophia. Doug Andrews would like you to come to his office, if you have a moment."

A call from the company president's executive assistant summoning me to his office? I was hoping this meant what I thought it meant. I hurried to Doug's office without trying to look like I was hurrying. If all went as expected, I was going to go home a very happy man tonight.

I had been waiting for news on this promotion to Product Director for weeks. It was my one and only chance to get on equal footing with the organizational thorn in my side. I've been working here at SysteMuscle for a few years, and I've earned this promotion already ... many times over. Doug Andrews recruited me to his company just as he was expanding his product lines of sporting equipment. We had met at a young professionals networking event. He was the featured speaker, talking about the new and exciting things going on at his start-up. He caught me at a lull in my career, taking up cubicle space at one of the big insurance companies in town. Doug and I hit it off instantly, and he came to trust me very quickly with more and more responsibility as his company continued to grow. The first few years at SysteMuscle were exhilarating. I was thrilled about coming to work every day, and I finally felt like my work had significance and meaning. Doug responded to my enthusiasm with a couple of major promotions and numerous raises and bonuses during those early years. Life was good.

Around my third anniversary with the company, a woman in her mid-forties unexpectedly stopped by my office. Her spiked and overly-colored hair gave her the appearance of a round, orange porcupine. When she opened her mouth, the porcupine persona just spilled into her personality. In a matronly, condescendingly, and overly polite fashion, she introduced herself as Rona Povo, Doug's new "lieutenant" and informed me I would be moving to a desk on the floor because she needed an office. I laughed in her face and told her I didn't have time for silly posturing. "If you want an office, wait in line," was my response. In hindsight, I could have handled it better. Two minutes later, I received an e-mail from Doug telling me I would have to move by the end of the day and I owed Rona an apology. Afterwards, Doug became more and more elusive, unless he or Rona wanted something. Then, it seemed, I was his buddy for the day. Rona never made requests herself, but she knew I would never tell Doug "no" so she always channeled all of her requests through him. It's hard to explain, but it seemed whenever anything went wrong (and there were a lot of things which mysteriously went wrong after she started at the company), Rona always seemed to be lurking around the corner … far enough away to avoid blame, but close enough I could sense her influence. Such was the office dynamic for the last couple of years.

I had considered quitting soon after Rona's arrival. I began looking for another job, but two things happened in quick succession. First, my wife decided to take a leave of absence from her job so she could go back to school for her master's degree. She begged me to "stay the course" so she wouldn't have to worry about our financial security and could focus on her schooling. My family instincts kicked in, as I knew I needed to play the provider role for her sake. About the same time, a couple other major employers in town went out of business in the soft economy, flooding the market with good employees and not enough jobs for them to fill. Therefore, I knew I'd better stay put. And as each day passed, I watched myself become more and more miserable.

A few weeks ago, the Product Director position opened up in a new line of business, and I jumped at the opportunity. Product directors were treated like royalty within SysteMuscle, and it was my one chance of getting on equal footing with Rona. I was hoping this meeting with Doug was the result of my efforts to accomplish this feat.

Doug motioned for me to have a seat when I reached his office. Because of the most recent growth spurt of the company, Doug and Rona had completed the addition of a new executive wing to the headquarters building, where they shared an executive assistant and adjoining offices. I could tell immediately from the look on his face the news was not going to be pleasant. I just had no idea how unpleasant it was going to be.

"We just think you're not quite ready to handle the responsibility of Product Director. Please understand, if the decision were up to me alone, I would have given it to you in a heartbeat, but I am accountable to other executives now that our company has grown," Doug continued to drone as I started to tune him out. He piled on excuse after excuse to make it sound plausible, at least to himself. I reengaged in listening as he was finishing up. "I'm not saying it will never happen, Toby. We just want you to prove yourself on this critical initiative before we make any rash assessments about your advancement."

Of course, all he could tell me about the critical initiative is that I'd be working with a team from the company's Call Center to improve some processes. Doug has never been one for details, unless they are spoon-fed to him, so I knew better than to press him for any additional information.

"Oh, before I forget," Doug summarized in a voice that was

more excited than the events called for, "you'll be answering to Rona Povo on this project. I'm promoting her to Executive VP of Operations, so she'll be handling a lot of the day-to-day operations to free me up to address other business pursuits. She's very interested in working with you on this project, since it appears our Call Center has not really kept up with the rest of the organization. Rona has hand-selected each member of your team. You'll be doing the whole management team a favor by handling this. After all, for what we pay our Call Center, I can outsource the whole thing to India." Doug chuckled as he fondled a desk model of his new speed boat.

I left his office numb. To make matters worse, Rona ran into me as I was leaving, giving her an opportunity to add her own acerbic slant to the assignment. Rona could take any negative emotion and make it worse. She reiterated what Doug had said, obviously delighted that she held such power over my career. She also made it perfectly clear that any screw-ups would have dire consequences for my future. After two minutes with her, if I had a tail, it would have been tucked between my legs as I slowly made my way back to my desk.

Then I did what I always did when something was going disastrously wrong in my life: I called my cousin Rex and asked him to meet me at our normal spot.

Chapter 1

"When the student is ready, the teacher will appear."

-Buddhist Proverb

"So, what's your big news?" I asked, hoping the change of subject would get me off the hook from the current topic.

"Nice try, Toby," came the reply from Rex. "But since you asked, I've just been promoted to Lieutenant of our local force. One of my new responsibilities is the commander of our department's SWAT team."

"SWAT Team? You mean like 'Special Weapons And Tactics'? You mean like bashing down doors and wearing camo and carrying big guns? That kind of SWAT?" I was genuinely excited for him. Rex had worked hard on the force for almost twenty years. He had served as a member of the SWAT team for over ten years. This was a big deal.

"Down, boy," Rex said with a laugh. "You're making the job sound a lot more glamorous than it is."

"Are you kidding?" I responded, almost uncharacteristically energetic. "That'd be my dream job! You get to make loud explosions and fight bad guys and solve crimes and put criminals behind bars. Being in charge of SWAT would absolutely rock!" My boyish enthusiasm was definitely in high gear. I'd always been fascinated by Rex's work in law enforcement. He was a few years older than I was. Being from a large, close-knit family, our relationship was actually more like brothers than cousins. As such, few people knew me better than he did. Usually, it felt great to have this level of transparency. Today, it wasn't really working in my favor.

"You're just saying that because you hate your current job." Rex was right to a degree. "However, you're overstating our role. SWAT has pretty tight boundaries."

"What do you mean?"

"Our job, in a nutshell, is to secure the stronghold."

"What's a stronghold?"

"Sorry… 'cop talk.' The stronghold is the house or building we're trying to make safe, but the point is we know where our job starts and stops. It starts when we get the call. It ends when we have all of the people in the stronghold secured."

"Secured?" I was starting to sound like we were playing twenty questions. Rex has always been patient with my inquisitiveness, and today was no different.

"Everyone in the building is either in custody or delivered to safety. But again, our emphasis is clearing the way for the detectives to come in and investigate whatever crime has been committed. Our job ends when the building is safe; investigation isn't our job. While we can't screw up things for the detectives, it's still very important we know where our responsibilities start and stop."

"Still … at least you get to do something stimulating." It was all I could come up with in the way of keeping my job out of the line of fire. And I was a little jealous he did an exciting and significant job.

"I'll tell you what, Toby," Rex said, an assuring smile on his face. "We have scenario training coming up a week from Saturday. Some developers will be tearing down a farm house near here, and they've told us we can practice entries there before it's demolished. I'll talk to my captain to see if it's okay, but would you like to come and watch us practice?"

"I'm pretty sure I'm open next Saturday, Rex," I answered, stirred at the prospect of getting to watch a real SWAT team in action.

"I'll send you details after I get the go-ahead from the captain. We sometimes have observers, so it's nothing new to us. You just have to promise to stay out of the way."

"It's a deal!" I was about to burst. This was the first great thing to happen to me in weeks.

Then Rex did what I feared he would do: he turned the topic of conversation back to me. "You never mentioned why you wanted to meet today," he baited me.

"Well," I paused for an uncomfortably long time. "It's about the transfer and promotion I applied for."

"Are congratulations in order for you as well?" Rex asked with anticipation in his voice. He knew how badly I wanted this promotion.

"Well … um … not exactly," I responded to the perplexed look on his face, and stumbled over finding the words to tell him about my past few days.

"Wait a second here … a new assignment instead of a promotion?" Rex cast an unconvinced look in my general direction.

"Well, Doug said it'd only be a matter of time before the promotion occurs. There were some senior managers who weren't comfortable giving it to me."

"'Some' senior managers … or Rona?" That one hurt. Rex knew about the relationship with Rona Povo ... mainly because I've vented about her weekly since I first met her. Although SysteMuscle, Inc. continued to grow larger and larger, it did not prevent me from crossing Rona's path all too frequently … usually with disastrous results.

"Doug wouldn't tell me specifically who it was." My response was technically accurate, but Rex had a knack for reading me like a book. It didn't help he was one of the sharpest police officers on the force. I could tell Rex's "protective older sibling" instincts were kicking in, so I mentally braced myself for the inevitable.

"Doug has dangled a lot of carrots in front of you over the last several years. Don't you think it's time to explore your options a little more?"

"I know where you're coming from, but I think …." I wasn't going to get to finish the sentence.

"All I'm saying is I think Doug is using you. You've been his go-to guy since starting at the company. Whenever there's an emergency, whenever he or Rona screw things up with a client, whenever there's a mess, you're their default solution. But they treat you like crap when it comes to rewarding you for your efforts."

Rex knew I was miserable with the situation, and his advice was only intended to help. For some reason, his next question really annoyed me.

"So, have you updated your resume?"

I had to give Rex credit; he was very direct.

"No." My reply was simple.

"And why, might I ask, haven't you told Doug where he could get off? You're between projects right now. You have a solid reputation throughout town. You can go anywhere you want. Help me understand your loyalty to this place." Rex was curious, but with an undertone of irritation.

I shrugged. I do that a lot more these days, it seems. It's becoming my trademark response when I don't have a better answer … another thing that's lacking in my life.

"Since you insist on moving forward with this insanity, what are your next steps with your new project?" Rex brought new meaning to the word tenacity.

"Um … not sure … I guess just meet with the team tomorrow morning and figure out what's wrong. How hard can it be?"

"Do you have any kind of game plan? Do you know who's on your team? Do you know what kinds of processes they work on? Have you thought about how you're going to document them?" Rex was making me nervous with all of these questions

… and rightfully so. I realized I had never really done any kind of formal activities around improving somebody's job or a department's work processes before. Worse yet, I hadn't asked any of these questions of Doug at the time. All I knew was I would be working with three line supervisors and a technical analyst from the Call Center Department.

"Er … well … I just thought we'd make it up as we go along," I was fumbling big-time, and Rex knew it. Instead of getting frustrated with me, though, he offered his advice and expertise.

"Sounds like somebody has an accomplishment deficit disorder," scoffed Rex.

"I said I'd get it figured out. I'm just not sure how I'll do it yet." I paused and shifted uncomfortably. "You have any ideas for corralling a Call Center project that's destined for failure before it even starts?"

"My guess is you'd better get a handle on what you are trying to accomplish."

"There's that word again: accomplishment." To be honest, just the word itself was irritating me. "If accomplishment is the key to all of this, then how do I get there? I'm a little stuck in my world of lack-of-accomplishment."

"Fair enough. The police department gives us many learning opportunities. Over the past few years, I've been taking a lot of command leadership classes. I learned some great things I've used both on patrol and with SWAT. There's one gem which has stuck out more than anything else. Have you ever heard of systems thinking?"

"Systems thinking? You mean computer stuff?"

"Not just computer stuff, although it applies. Systems thinking means looking at every process in your organization in a new way. Everything you do in your company is to accomplish something, so you need to look at these tasks as if they're all related. Do you think about every action you take as having an impact further down the road? Can you take the results and outputs you get and reverse your way through the system to identify which inputs helped you yield those results? There's the heart of systems thinking."

"Well, I know how to build a flow-chart ... does that count?" I didn't like getting management advice from my cousin. I'm not sure why it was bothering me. It just was.

"It depends," Rex didn't let up. "What're you going to do with the flowchart once you've made it? Do you know exactly what you're documenting? Do you know why you're capturing the processes? In short, do you know what you want to accomplish?"

"I suppose ... If I knew it would really make a difference ... I don't 'do futility' well. Rona has something up her sleeve, and I'm not really sure what it is, but this assignment is far from a reward, and Doug's conveniently unavailable unless he wants something. Besides, we weren't talking about me anymore; we were talking about systems ... the non-computer kind."

"Yes we were. You know the phrase 'garbage in, garbage out' right?" I nodded. "You've also heard the phrase 'you reap what you sow,' haven't you?" Again, I agreed. "OK, those are both examples of systems thinking. And it works in every single business or organization, including your sporting goods company and including my police department."

"Refresh my memory ... I know I've seen this in some class or seminar in my past, but what does a system look like?"

Rex then removed a notebook from his shirt pocket and grabbed a pen. I noticed the SWAT team used their own customized notebooks. On the sheet, he drew the following and handed it to me:

S.W.A.T. FLYER

Everything is a system

inputs transformation outputs

feedback

environment

"SWAT Flyer?" I smirked.

"OK, bad word play on fly-swatter, but you're focusing on the wrong part of the page," he scolded me.

"It looks pretty straightforward," I stated blankly.

"Looks can be deceiving," Rex noted. "Think about your new assignment from a systems standpoint. What is the desired output? Like I said before, what do you want to accomplish?"

"A promotion for me." I wasn't going to make this easy on Rex. He didn't bite, and he wasn't going to make it any easier on me.

"Fair enough. What are the inputs which'll get you that promotion?"

"Hmmm ... good performance on this project ... no, make it stellar performance on this project ... from me and my team."

"How will your feedback loop define stellar performance on the project?"

"A workable solution with a good rate of return." I recited dutifully from all of the company meetings I'd sat through where Doug lectured us on corporate values, goals, strategies, blah, blah, blah.

"What would make it a workable solution? How will you

know you've achieved your output?"

"I guess I'll find out tomorrow. I meet with my team for the first time in the morning. I've heard from some of my friends in the company that the customer service crowd is ... um... unique."

"What do you mean?" Rex was never one for ambiguous answers, which I should have known by now.

"They have a reputation for being a little difficult with outsiders." It was truly all I had heard, but the message had come consistently from multiple sources during my career. I hoped it was just hearsay, but I had a sneaking suspicion the people on the front lines of SysteMuscle were about to teach me some very difficult lessons before this was all finished.

"Well, there's another input you'll have to contend with," Rex observed.

"Since when is human behavior a system input?" I looked inquisitive.

"Since when isn't it?" Rex countered. "Remember, everything—and I do mean EVERYTHING—going into the process to accomplish your solution is an input. And even if you want your solution to be the kind of output you desire, you still may have to deal with some unwanted inputs. Difficult behaviors are inputs too many managers overlook."

"How so?"

"We once hired a cop who looked great on paper. Excellent records. Perfect physical fitness. Highest marks for education. It didn't take us long to figure out the guy was a complete jerk. Nobody wanted to partner with him. Nobody trusted him. Even the union steward turned his back on him. The chief had to let him go, because his behavior had become so destructive to morale. It was an unfortunate feedback loop, but the outputs justified it."

"SysteMuscle never fires anybody," I mused. "I may be the first if Rona has her way."

"You'll be fine," Rex assured me. "Just keep your nose

clean and try using some systems thinking to design your accomplishments. I've got your back … after all, we Donovan boys stick together, right? We'll talk about this more later. I gotta run, but I'll ask the Captain about letting you observe our SWAT training next week." With a cavalier smile, he tossed the SWAT Flyer pad in front of me. "Here, keep this. You may want to take notes."

And then he was gone. After Rex left, I turned to the next page in the SWAT Flyer pad and wrote:

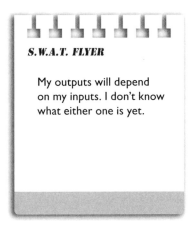

S.W.A.T. FLYER

My outputs will depend on my inputs. I don't know what either one is yet.

Usually my talks with Rex leave me feeling more confident and self-assured. So why was I suddenly feeling really lousy?

Chapter 2

"This time, like all times, is a very good one, if we but know what to do with it."

-Ralph Waldo Emerson

I felt a chill as I walked into the conference room at SysteMuscle the following morning, and it had nothing to do with the thermostat setting. Seated around the table were four stone figures, monuments to angry gods with stone cold stares which could make the bravest explorer cower. Okay, so they were real people, not stone statues, but the sentiment was there. The Customer Service Call Center department at SysteMuscle was generally kept at arm's length from other company operations, and they had complained for years about this treatment. The breakdown of communications was about to come back to bite me. From the moment I opened my mouth to begin introductions, I was accosted with all of the reasons why these meetings (and I) were both unneeded and unwanted. For each comment they made, my mind was racing with its own questions and comments.

"Why are we doing this again?" (What? Didn't anybody tell them why?)

"Didn't the other consulting firm do this to us last year?"

(What other consulting firm?)

"Yeah, what happened to their flow charts?" (Great, I'm reinventing the wheel.)

"Flow charts? You're going to make us create more flow charts?" (Yeah, I like unnecessary work as well as you do.)

"Are we going to use Six Sigma or Lean? I was told we'd actually get to use a real methodology." (Just what I needed, a process geek who's hung up on tools.)

"Is it true you're only doing this so you can outsource our positions to India and shut down the Call Center?" (How did that information leak out?)

"What do you know about Call Centers?" (Virtually nothing, as long as we're being honest.)

"For that matter, what do you know about our customers?" (Ouch! That one hurt, given how long I've been with the company.)

"Do I really need to be here? I have real work to do at my desk." (And so the truth comes out. They don't perceive this as real work.)

I stumbled over answers to their questions—feeble attempts, really—and I could tell my hopes of attaining credibility quickly were walking a very high tightrope. And the tightrope had no net beneath it while the stone gods had gathered on either end of the rope to start jiggling.

First, I acknowledged I was unaware they had been put through this exercise before. Doug and Rona had made it sound like I was going to be doing the company some huge favor. Rona also had a knack for spinning any situation to make it sound better than it actually was. Many times, she made assignments sound really good just to get somebody lured in. Then BAM—the bait-and-switch occurred! Employees started referring to her as the "Venus Lie-Trap" because she had tricked so many people into bad projects. As the team was quick to inform me, it turned out there had been a couple of attempts to improve the customer service processes in this area. The first consultant had quit abruptly, citing "irreconcilable differences" with the team as she quickly left the building in tears. Last year, Doug had brought in one of the high end East Coast consulting firms to again tackle this task. When the team challenged them, the consultants ignored them completely and came up with their own recommendations and processes. Members of the department were so mad at the consultants they went out of their way to sabotage the recommendations so as to ensure failure. I gulped hard when I heard this piece of news.

So ... they had been through this type of thing before. Rona had said she wanted to start with a clean slate and a fresh set of eyes. I wasn't sure if she did this because of her lack of confidence in the other consultants Doug had hired, if this was some kind of power play on her part, or if she was salivating at the thought of my falling flat on my face. I decided to ask the team if any of them had the papers or charts from the other consultants, since it seemed foolish at least not to look at these prior efforts. A woman named Rachel Humeston pulled out a folder and slid it across the table toward me. Rachel was pretty caustic and outspoken so far, and her body language was closed: arms crossed, legs crossed, hands clasped ... if it meant what I thought it meant, this assignment could be a pretty nasty endurance test.

"Good luck understanding those," she stated succinctly as I very quickly fanned through the 150-page document. I could see what she meant. What I saw was a lot of very technical writing and some highly complex charts which would make an engineering student shudder.

"Thanks," I mumbled. "Are these all of the charts and graphs and documents?"

"They're the only ones I could dig up on such short notice," Rachel responded. "Management doesn't believe in hanging onto things long. Most of the people who have worked on similar projects before these have either been 'selectively eliminated' or have left for greener pastures." She didn't seem bitter about this; rather, she stated it as objectively as if she were giving somebody traffic directions. At this point, I decided to take a slightly different route. I held up the stack Rachel had given me.

"Do you feel these papers accurately represent the input given during the prior sessions?"

"Well, no, not really," the response came from Evan Chambers, another supervisor from the Call Center. He was the oldest of the team of four, and he carried a marginal degree of authority with the others because of his age and seniority. His answer was echoed by nods and murmurs from the others in the room. I prompted him to elaborate, so he continued. "It seemed like the consultants came into the room with their flip charts and their scented markers and their sticky notes and told us how our process worked rather than asked us." The headshakes from earlier turned into vigorous nods of agreement. "Anytime one of us would try to tell them they were representing our process incorrectly, they would call a time out and go into a sidebar discussion. They'd come back and tell us their methodology was tried and true and successful with numerous Fortune 500 companies, and they were sure the problem was just a communication gap since our 'homey little company obviously didn't grasp the nuances of advanced levels of reengineering.'"

I cringed, for I knew that type of consulting firm well. In my department, we handle a lot of hiring and firing of contractors for various projects. I had come to despise the arrogance of those who were better at insulting than consulting. And even though I was also an employee, these Call Center supervisors perceived me as an outsider. What I didn't want was to be lumped into the same category. I somehow had to begin winning them over, or at least prevent them from growing more hostile.

"OK, here's the deal. If at any point you feel I'm not listening to you or not representing your ideas or feelings correctly, call me on it right then and there."

"Yeah, right ..." countered Seth Taran, another Call Center supervisor, and the youngest of the group. "So you can just go back to Rona and tell her we won't cooperate? Look, the only reason I'm here is I was told we might get to use some of the newer methodologies like Six Sigma, or Lean, or SCRUM. I've been in the local MBA program for months, and I've been aching to try these things. Rona told me we might get to on this project, so I signed up. By the looks of things, it doesn't sound like you know any of those tools, so let's just get this over with. You tell us what you want us to do, and we'll pretend to care. Fair enough?"

"Have it your way," I responded without hesitation. "But the offer still stands. When we get going, if you think I'm not paying attention to you, then tell Rona yourself. Trust me, if she thinks you don't like me, she'll be the first in line to fire me."

It wasn't much of an entry to go on, but it was all I had, so I laid out the plan of attack for them. Rona and Doug wanted better efficiencies from the Call Center. They also made it clear we were not to screw up anything else in the process. Knowing Rona, it was more of a dig on me than it was any kind of professional challenge. Either way, we needed to start somewhere, so I suggested we look at where they were right now, referring to it as their "as is" or current state.

"If what we're doing is wrong, why are we wasting time rehashing it?" Rachel perked up again. "It seems like we've been through this over and over again, and nothing ever gets decided or changed. No offense to you, Toby, but you're the outsider here. We live this stuff day in and day out, and if management wants us to change, we'll do what we always do: salute and comply. I'm just not sure rehashing the old is going to lead us to the new. Besides, I don't know what's so bad with how we're doing now. Our customers hate us, but we get a paycheck for the abuse."

Her comment was greeted with agreement around the table, and once again I was put on the defensive. I took a deep breath, and silently counted to ten before I spoke.

"Your concern is warranted," I responded to her. "If I had been through as many false starts as you say you've endured, the last thing I'd want to do is go through yet another person wanting me to start at the beginning. It would be like a police interrogation where you kept getting asked the same questions over and over again." I grinned to myself a little when I thought of how Rex would appreciate the analogy. But I was following through on my promise. Just by listening to Rachel and validating her concerns, she seemed to relax a little, so I kept talking, this time addressing Evan.

"Didn't you say none of the previous consultants ever showed an understanding of how you really do your job?" The comment had the desired effect, because they all had to admit there never had been a truly accurate analysis of how things currently worked within the Call Center. Even Rachel acknowledged I had a point. Then I continued, "One of the drawbacks of trying to improve processes and work is the people involved aren't starting out on the same page. Jumping into an improvement initiative without making sure everyone understands and agrees to how things currently work is like holding a race where the course is not charted out, and you're asking everybody to start from a different point, but you're not telling them where the finish line is."

"Around here, improvements are treated like the Supreme Court's definition of pornography: We can't define it but we'll know it when we see it," said Seth, whose comment drove home my point even more. "OK, how do you propose we approach your 'as is' or 'current state' or whatever it is you called it?"

Again, it wasn't much, but they were at least letting me move forward. I laid out my proposal to the team. We would first identify all of the processes we could—just figure out everything they do. Then we would build a checklist containing all of the processes and work our way through them one by one. We would step through each process and flowchart it out in a way which made sense for them and for me. I told them, as an outsider, I would be their "for dummies" test. If I didn't get it, we were making the process too complex.

I chuckled to myself as I thought back to the calendar on my desk. It's one of those one-management-quote-a-day deals, and this morning's quote was perfect for what I was going through.

Peter Drucker, the patron saint of people who work more with their brains than their hands, was quoted, "My greatest strength as a consultant is to be ignorant and ask a few questions." Either way, they'd at least see my ego wasn't getting in the way of their processes. Once we had the "as is" hammered out, we would start on building the "to be" or future state where we wanted to go.

Immediately, the struggles began in earnest as we attempted to identify the list of processes. Elena Gregg, the fourth member of the group, had yet to say anything substantial. As much as I prompted her, she merely declined with a simple "no thanks." I guessed she knew a lot more than she was letting on, and it didn't help that the other three weren't letting her get a word in edgewise. Still, there were a couple of times already when she appeared to want to add to the conversation, thought better of it, and remained the passive participant. Nevertheless, she looked more engaged than bored, so I decided I could write off the behavior for now as a personality thing and turned my attention to the other three who wouldn't stop talking. While their open hostility originally was directed at me, eventually they began to turn on each other. (At least I knew they were consistent.) Evan, being a big picture thinker, defined processes with broad sweeping strokes and generalities. Seth and Rachel were very detail oriented, and kept challenging Evan every time he opened his mouth. Finally, he just folded his arms and pushed his chair back from the table. Big warning flag! I knew I couldn't afford to lose Evan (or any of them, for that matter) at the very first meeting.

"Um … Evan," I began tentatively. "We still need you here."

"What?" he asked with an air of mock innocence. "I'm still in the room, aren't I?"

"Well, technically, yes," I responded, attempting to remain diplomatic. "However, your body language is telling me you may not be playing in the sandbox any more." I had hoped the analogy would lighten the mood, but it backfired when Rachel opened her mouth.

"Don't mind him," she interjected abruptly. "When little Evan doesn't get his way, he goes into a corner and pouts."

This unfiltered commentary set him off. His face flushed, he stood up to face Rachel. The vein on his forehead was noticeably throbbing, so it was obvious to all she had hit a hot button, one I guessed had been pushed many times before my arrival. He took a deep breath and opened his mouth to unleash his retort. A quick scan around the room made him change his mind. He shut his mouth, shut his planner, got up and pushed his chair back into the table (with audible force) and was headed toward the door.

"Evan, get back in here and sit down." I was generally unaccustomed to bossing around a stranger, especially on the first day, but I figured if Rona and Doug had thrown me into a lions' den, I wasn't going to get eaten alive without doing active battle with a few of the mangy beasts first. I certainly wasn't going to let them pull the passive-aggressive-sneaking-off-on-the-first-meeting trick.

He turned around and looked at me, obviously examining whether I had the intestinal fortitude to make him follow through on my command. I took advantage of the pause to shift the attention to the broader group.

"Look, everybody. You've all worked together before, and you all know each others' hot buttons. And some of you" (I glared briefly at Rachel) "are obviously not afraid to push them with disturbing frequency. We're going to be in these meetings together for a few weeks, so I suggest we get a few things in order right here and now."

I walked over to the nearest flip chart and wrote:

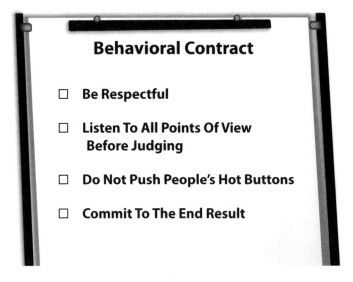

Behavioral Contract

☐ **Be Respectful**

☐ **Listen To All Points Of View Before Judging**

☐ **Do Not Push People's Hot Buttons**

☐ **Commit To The End Result**

I walked back over to Evan's chair and held it out for him, gestured for him to sit back down, and turned to the rest of the group.

"Your turn," I said, pointing to the list. "If we're going to be in here awhile, we're going to communicate respectfully. I was asked to do a job, and I'm not going to let your petty bickering get in the way. There's a time and a place for conflict, and it can be very healthy at moving a team forward. What I just observed was far from it, so we're going to create our own rules of engagement."

"How about learning how to balance details with big picture thinking?" Evan offered as he took his seat. I nodded as I wrote it on the chart with the others. The atmosphere in the room relaxed a little, and we continued for a few minutes to write up a few others, like showing up for meetings on time and turning off cell phones.

When the team wasn't looking, I pulled out the notebook Rex had given me and opened it to the first blank page. Very quickly, I wrote:

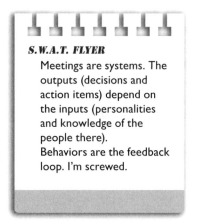

S.W.A.T. FLYER
Meetings are systems. The outputs (decisions and action items) depend on the inputs (personalities and knowledge of the people there).
Behaviors are the feedback loop. I'm screwed.

Once we agreed on how we would behave, we turned our attention back to the task at hand. We continued identifying processes, yet the team still seemed to struggle with where one process ended and another began. At this point, it seemed like a silly argument to get into, so I assured the group we could work through those particulars when we began tackling each process in detail, which generated yet another debate about exactly how detailed each process should be. Evan and Rachel's conflict from earlier seemed to be resurfacing, so I decided to head it off. Again, I emphasized we eventually would analyze the finer points of every process; for now we should just focus on identifying processes rather than defining them. After what seemed like a lengthier time than necessary, we finished brainstorming all of the easily identifiable processes and tried to group them into broader categories. After even more debate and discussion, the team figured out all of their identified processes fit into about eight general categories:

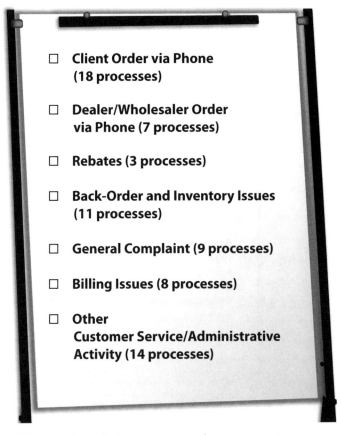

- ☐ **Client Order via Phone (18 processes)**

- ☐ **Dealer/Wholesaler Order via Phone (7 processes)**

- ☐ **Rebates (3 processes)**

- ☐ **Back-Order and Inventory Issues (11 processes)**

- ☐ **General Complaint (9 processes)**

- ☐ **Billing Issues (8 processes)**

- ☐ **Other Customer Service/Administrative Activity (14 processes)**

We went through the categories and processes again, just to ensure we all agreed. I decided after this marathon session, the group had experienced enough togetherness for one meeting. Before we broke up, we decided on the schedule for our next few meetings, giving everyone a chance to rearrange other commitments and also to complete any research or action items coming from this first meeting. We also divided up the processes and groupings among the team members to allow them to talk with their co-workers.

I received a few affirming smiles as people left the room, but they all seemed anxious to get out as quickly as possible. As I collected flip chart papers and other supplies, I was wondering how fast I could update my resume. There had to be a better way of getting this collection of individuals to agree on the processes which would allow us to improve how the Call Center would work in the future; I just wasn't sure what it was.

I again pulled out the notepad Rex had given me and thought about what I had observed today.

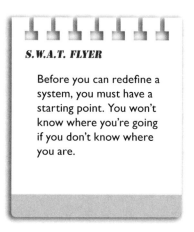

S.W.A.T. FLYER

Before you can redefine a system, you must have a starting point. You won't know where you're going if you don't know where you are.

I was deflated as I walked back to my desk. When I sat down, I found an e-mail from Rex. It's great he knows me so well; he must have been channeling my frustration.

FROM: Lt. Rex Donovan
TO: Toby Donovan
SUBJECT: Systems Thinking
DATE: 23 July

Toby:

Hope your first session today went well … was doing some reading from Peter Senge's *The Fifth Discipline* and wondered if this could be some encouragement to you in your current "predicament":

> "If organizations have an "attention span" of only one or two years (some might say one or two months), is it impossible to learn things that might require five or ten years? … In a recent session of a five-day introductory course for member companies in the MIT Learning Center, an engineering manager from Ford framed the core issue succinctly: "After a few days," she said, "I am beginning to 'get' what this systems thinking and mental models stuff is all about. It reminds me of when I first studied calculus. At first, I was totally lost. Calculus was a new way of thinking for me. But then I started to 'get it.' Within a year, I had mastered the basics. Within five years it was part of my professional capabilities." She then added, "If calculus were invented today, none of our corporations could learn it. We'd send everyone off to the three-day course. We'd then give them three months to try it out and see if 'it worked.' After it had failed, we'd conclude it was of little value and move on to something else." (Fifth Discipline, Introduction)

I hope this sheds some light on my comments about systems thinking. Just be patient; good things will happen.

Also, the Captain said "YES" to letting you watch us next Saturday. I'll call with the address. It's not too far from where you live. Plan on being there around 8 AM.

Props
Rex

And there it was, right in front of me on my screen. What these people needed was not a new problem. They needed my patience and understanding as they accomplished a new solution to an old problem.

Chapter 3

"Most of us are about as eager to be changed as we were to be born, and go through our changes in a similar state of shock."

-James Baldwin

Getting this group to agree on anything was challenging at best. Our next meeting saw us beginning to map out the current processes of the Call Center for SysteMuscle. While I persuaded the team to start flowcharting with the existing processes, they still were not convinced.

In an effort to make the flowcharting easier for all of us, I did a little research on some different ways of creating flowcharts. The best method I found—at least, the one which made the most sense in the short time available—was called a deployment flowchart, or a swim-lane diagram. These charts emphasize the people performing the work over the work itself. Given that accountability appeared to be an issue in the Call Center at SysteMuscle, this was probably going to be our best route.

As the fearsome foursome (as I called them) filed into the room, they were greeted by a wall full of plain, brown, butcher block paper and a stack of adhesive notepads.

Seth began the mockery by picking up a notepad and playfully flinging it across the table at Rachel. "Oh great, Toby wants to play consultant. Look! He even brought pretty colored paper."

"We may as well get this over with," sighed Rachel. "The sooner we tell them how we want to change things, the sooner they'll tell us we're wrong, and things can stay the same."

"I don't know about you, but I already have a screen full of e-mails from unhappy customers," Evan complained. "Some of you may view this as an excuse to get out of work, but I'd rather be at my desk."

I looked at Elena, who remained silent. "Anything you'd like to add?" I invited in my warmest voice possible. She merely smiled and shook her head. There was definitely more there than she was letting on. Elena was non-verbally engaged. She smiled and frowned at all the right spots in the conversation. From what I could tell, she was on my side, even though she said nothing. Her body language showed she was displeased with the dysfunctional behavior of her coworkers. I knew she'd have to contribute at some point, but getting her there might take some effort.

"Great," I continued with little fanfare and even less patience. "As you made very clear in our last meeting, you don't want to be here. Well, we're stuck with each other. So I'm going to make you an offer you can't refuse."

"Who does this guy think he is? The Godfather?" Rachel muttered to Evan. Normally I would have ignored the comment, but it was too good to pass up.

"As a matter of fact, I am a fan of the movie," I admitted as Rachel blushed at being caught. "And to help you remember the steps to flowcharting, let me introduce you to BRANDO."

To much eye-rolling and muttering, I outlined the process we would be using to create the flowcharts. Seth's eyes lit up when I mentioned the swim-lane charts as these were a common tool used by Six Sigma teams.

I then proceeded to explain the steps for building a swim-lane chart:

1. **Boundaries:** Identify where each process starts and stops

2. **Roles:** Identify the general categories of responsibility

3. **Activity:** Identify the individual steps in the process - each action goes in a rectangle and each decision point goes in a diamond

4. **Negotiate:** Review the steps for accuracy, clarity, and validation

5. **Draw:** Finish connecting the lines among boxes to pull the system together

6. **Opportunities:** Discuss and look for areas for improvement

Rather than leave it open for them to argue about which process to tackle first, I made an executive decision for them, and announced we would begin with the process they had called "customer places order—single item/product line."

"The first step is to identify the boundaries where the process starts and stops." I thought about what Rex had told me about his job on the SWAT team being very clear on this point. "Anyone want to offer a suggestion?"

"I would guess it starts when a customer decides to buy something from us and picks up the phone," Rachel tossed out.

"And it ends when one of them sends me an e-mail

complaining about their experience," interjected Evan.

I raised one eyebrow at him and gave him "the look."

"OK, OK," he conceded. "I guess it really ends when the Shipping and Fulfillment Department takes over the order."

"Should we flowchart the process of how they lose and/or otherwise screw up the order?" asked Seth.

"Is it really a problem?" I inquired.

Seth turned to Evan and Rachel and stated in a soft voice just loud enough for me to hear, "See? I told you he was out of touch with how things really work around here." Then he turned to me and audibly condescended, "Yes, it's a problem. But I doubt you or Rona or Doug want to fix it."

"Doug? Does he still even work here?" Rachel seemed bemused by her own comment. It was warranted, though. Doug had become more and more of an absentee executive ever since Rona showed up on the scene.

"OK, so the process starts with the customer initiating an order," I redirected the conversation, "and it ends with the order being passed off to Shipping and Fulfillment, correct?"

All four nodded their heads with varying degrees of enthusiasm. At least Elena is capable of some type of communication, I thought. What is her story? Why is she here?

"This covers the first step. Alright, moving right along, who is involved in this process?" I decided to keep them focused.

"It depends on who is taking the order. Duh!" Seth's attitude was starting to get on my nerves and we were only ten minutes into the meeting. I took a deep breath and let it out slowly before I responded.

"I mean, Seth, what are the various roles involved? As you just so graciously pointed out, if we wrote down everybody's name, we'd be here for quite a while, wouldn't we? For this process, though, there's the customer, one of the Customer Service Representatives, and …" I wrote those two roles along the left-hand side of one of the long strips of paper, then prompting them for more ideas, I asked, "Who else?"

"The Credit Department may get involved if this is a customer we've had problems with in the past," Rachel interjected. "We also have to check the Inventory Control System to see if what they want is in stock." I added both of those to the list beneath the first two.

"Occasionally, one of us supervisors has to get involved if we have an irate customer or an incompetent rep," Evan offered.

"Really?" I countered. "Are our customers irate as they are placing orders? Why don't they just go elsewhere?"

"SysteMuscle has some long standing relationships with certain dealers, but those relationships don't make them any happier to deal with us. Granted, it's rare when it happens, but it does still occur." I shrugged at Evan's explanation and wrote the additional role below the others.

"I guess Shipping and Fulfillment would be the last role involved, although they just receive what we send them," Seth was playing along, at least for now.

"But they do come back and ask for clarification if there's a problem with the order," Rachel added. "They don't begin processing until they're sure we have it right. Remember the big argument last quarter between their supervisors and ours?"

"What was that about?" I was genuinely curious.

"They were constantly shipping a certain item wrong, and Evan was hearing about it. He sent them a list of all the orders containing the item and the complaints he was receiving. They had changed the item name and the part number in their database without telling anybody else," Rachel explained. "They told us we should have known about it, but there was never any communication on it, so we argued with them. The whole thing was escalated up to Rona and then to Doug."

"Word of advice," Evan stated dryly. "Never escalate a customer issue to somebody whose name is the phonetic cross-section of 'duh' and 'ugh.' He didn't do anything except make matters worse and leave it for Rona to clean up. She just ended up making everybody so angry we had to join forces with Shipping and Fulfillment to deal with her, and we forgot the argument."

"I think I remember," I vaguely recalled a few days last quarter when Rona was particularly out of sorts and was vocalizing her common threat of outsourcing "the whole damn company, especially those idiots in the Call Center and Shipping." Again, I found myself redirecting the conversation. So, these are the roles involved in this process, right?"

Process Order - Single Product Line	
Customer	
Cust Svc Rep (CSR)	
Credit	
ICKE	
Supervisor	
Shipping & Fulfillment	

When the team understood where I was headed, they at least pretended to give me their attention. They nodded their agreement, and motioned for me to keep going.

"So, you said the first step in the process was the customer phoning you with an order," I reiterated the earlier comment and wrote the step on one of the rectangular sticky notes and posted it in the customer swim-lane. "Now what happens?"

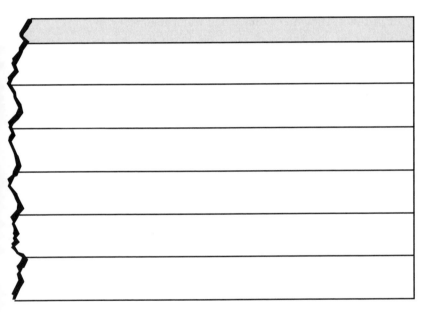

"According to the CSR manual," Rachel ceremoniously pulled out the three-inch binder and plopped it on the table with a loud thud, "the rep is supposed to validate the customer's credit history and verify their information. Then they're supposed to check the inventory system to make sure what the customer wants is in stock." I started to write the rectangles on the note pad when Seth unexpectedly began waving his arms in wild animation.

"Seth?" I acknowledged. "Do you have something to add, or are you short-circuiting?" I figured he had it coming, given the difficult time he'd given me so far. He merely scowled at the innuendo.

"Rachel is wrong," he blurted out, immediately creating a defensive atmosphere in the room. "On my team, we check inventory first and then validate the customer's credit and information."

"I'm wrong?" Rachel glared at Seth across the table. "This from the man who's so busy studying every fly-by-night management fad he's too busy to do real work. Look, you've only been supervising a Call Center team for six months; I've been doing it for fifteen years ..."

"Then you've been doing it wrong for fifteen years," he retorted.

"Time Out!" I interjected firmly before letting them go too far off track. "Rachel, obviously your way is documented in the manual. Does everybody follow this sequence, and is there a reason it has to be done in a specific order?"

Rachel opened her mouth to speak, but it was as though the response was uncomfortably lodged in her throat, and no crowbar would loosen it. She just seemed shocked and angry anybody would dare to challenge her publicly on a Call Center process. "We'll get back to you," I told her unapologetically, as I turned to Seth. "Why is your way good enough to bypass the documented process?"

"Isn't it obvious?!" he struck back with an air of exasperation. He calmed down a little to explain further. "Look, we screw

44

up the customer validation process a lot because of outdated information on their records. We're also on back-order on certain popular items. If we're out of stock, why bother putting the customer through the aggravation of validating their information? We'd just end up annoying them twice." Seth's explanation made sense. Evan and Elena both had a look of surprised revelation at the rationale. Rachel just sulked.

"If you had to poll all the customer service reps, how many of them do it Seth's way as opposed to what's in the manual?" I directed the question at all four of them. Everyone on Seth's team—about ten CSRs—checked inventory first. Evan admitted there was probably a mix of ways of doing it, and he didn't track the process to this level of detail, to which Elena just nodded. Rachel was adamant everybody did it by the book on her team, or they were written up if caught deviating from standards.

"And there's the catch," Seth was determined to come out on top.

"And what's that supposed to mean?" Rachel was already seething. She was used to pushing other people's buttons, but being openly confronted was not something she relished.

"You only think your team is following your lead," Seth continued his attack on Rachel. "When you're not watching, they do whatever they want. You can't micromanage a team of fifteen reps every single minute of every single day … especially not in this place."

"What do you know about how I manage my team?" Rachel's voice went up an octave. This was getting ugly, typical for a meeting with this group.

"Well, Rachel, he …" Evan was cut off by her smoldering glare.

"May I interrupt?" I asked as calmly and politely as I could.

"You've been an interruption since our first meeting … why stop now?" When Rachel was mad, everybody became a potential target for her verbal venom. I resolved not to let it bother me.

"First, at our last meeting we made a contract about how we would all try to behave. So far, you've broken about half of the points we agreed to. Second, on the issue about what order things happen … does it really matter? What I mean is whether the end result will be the same regardless of what order these specific steps occur?"

"I suppose," she mumbled after a prolonged and uncomfortable silence.

"If it helps, I'll document the process the way it appears in the manual," I offered, "but I'll also put a note in my report that indicates half of the reps do these two steps in the opposite order." The compromise seemed to appease everybody, so we moved on from this crisis. The calm was short-lived.

"By the way, Toby, I noticed you've been calling it the Inventory Control System," Evan brought up the point innocently enough. "The actual name of the system is ICKE—the Inventory Control Knowledge Entity."

"Yeah, but nobody calls it ICKE … which is a stupid name, by the way," argued Seth. "We all just call it the Inventory Control System or ICS."

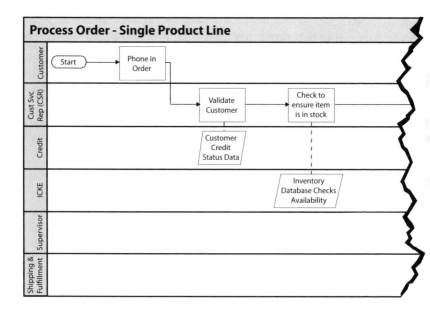

"This could explain why Shipping gets confused every time your team sends a note with an order," gruffed Evan. "For them, ICS stands for Interstate Commerce System. Do you realize how many errors I've headed off because you just throw out any old acronym instead of using the proper terminology?"

"They know what I mean," Seth shot back. "Quit being so anal. You're starting to sound like Rachel."

And so it went. Argument after argument. Rectangle after rectangle. Page after excruciating page. They argued about when to place a decision diamond in the flowchart to show where it forked off into two different paths. They argued about the frequency of each decision path. At least this argument was thwarted by having data reports available, because in the conflict of drama vs. data, drama may win a few battles, but data almost always wins the war.

By the end of the first meeting, we had one lonely process documented. The start of the process looked like this when we were done:

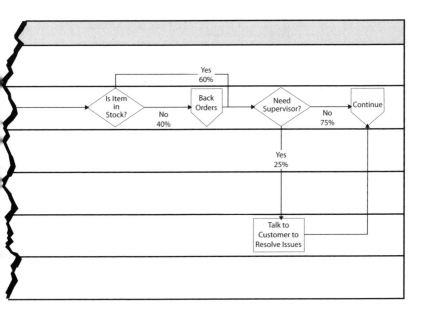

On the way out the door, Rachel capped off her bad mood with one final jab at me, "If you want me to continue wasting my time with these lessons in futility, you're going to have to make a little better case for why we need to change our processes in the first place. Our company is doing fine as is, and I haven't seen any real reason to make it better."

"While I hate to admit it, she has a point," Seth sneered at both Rachel and me. "This flowcharting stuff is child's play. I don't get why we have to waste our time when Rona's the only one who seems to have a problem."

I looked to Evan for help, and he just shrugged. My apparent apathy must be contagious. Elena merely smiled sympathetically as she exited. To make matters worse, Rona caught me on the way back to my desk. When I admitted we had documented one single process so far, she gave me a bemused little smile accompanied by an over-dramatized sigh.

"I guess Doug is going to owe me a steak dinner after all. I tried to tell him you just weren't ready for this level of responsibility. Let's see if you can pick up the pace just a little. At this rate, I can only imagine how you'll look when your team presents their findings to the executive committee on the first of September."

"September 1st, Rona? You told me the team could take as much time as we needed to ensure we got it right."

"Oh, no-no-no-no-no, Toby. I would've never told you that, or you'd be taking your own sweet time … as you're obviously doing now. Your team will be presenting in just five weeks. I guess it will be a good opportunity to demonstrate to Doug his judgment has been clouded in keeping you on his payroll this long. Have a delightful day." She managed to emphasize the last sentence in an icy drawl which made my skin crawl.

As she was leaving, the elevator opened behind me and I heard the muzak version of the Brent Burns' country-western song "Mean People Suck" lilting out into the hall. Hmmm … who knew Rona came with a sound track?

As had become my habit after just a couple of meetings, I was trying to document my observations in my SWAT Flyer notebook. I thought back over today's meeting and went through a couple of pages of observation:

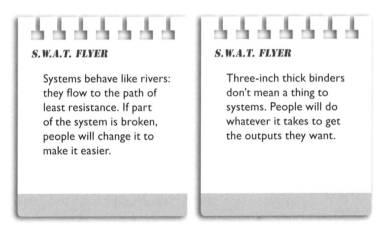

S.W.A.T. FLYER	S.W.A.T. FLYER
Systems behave like rivers: they flow to the path of least resistance. If part of the system is broken, people will change it to make it easier.	Three-inch thick binders don't mean a thing to systems. People will do whatever it takes to get the outputs they want.

I met Rex at our usual watering hole after work. My body language spoke volumes … mainly, I was a man defeated. Still, as bad as I felt, I was thrilled about spending the next day with Rex and his team, so I tried to hide my own issues. Rex saw right through this charade immediately, and I ended up giving him the recap of the day's meeting.

"Well, shouldn't it be pretty easy to just define how things work now? How hard can it be for a team to tell you how they do their jobs and put it down on paper?" Rex's questions seemed legit, but if he only knew how things really worked in our company.

"You'd think so, wouldn't you?" It was all I chose to throw out for a response.

"But …"

"But, what?" I've never been able to pull off an air of innocence.

"Don't toy with me. I'm a cop."

Busted.

"OK, it's like this: SysteMuscle is successful in spite of itself. Changes are slammed through without giving any thought as to why they're needed. Nobody thinks about results and outcomes unless something goes wrong. Then, instead of hunting for solutions, it becomes a hunt for blame, which is also subjective and all depends on who can smear the others better. Nobody does anything based on facts, figures, or data."

"Sounds kind of like the police department, except we document everything," Rex grinned. Then he added mischievously, "It makes the hunt for guilty parties a lot easier later."

"Brilliant. Maybe you can take over this team."

"My intuition is telling me it's not the team or the assignment dragging you down."

"OK, if you must know, what is really bugging the heck out of me is Rona Povo."

"What'd she do now?"

"This whole thing was a set-up. When I got this assignment, she told me we'd have as much time as we needed. Then today, after the meeting, she informed me we're presenting to Doug and the Board of Directors on September 1st. That's only five weeks away! Worse yet, she actually admitted to me she wants me to fail so she can convince Doug to fire me."

"Worse things could happen …" Rex muttered.

"Look, I know you think I should've left this company when they hired her. You also know why I stayed. Can we change the subject?"

"Not yet," Rex replied. "You still have today on your mind, and we're not going to be able to talk about anything else until you're able to process this. What were your two biggest roadblocks today? If you can articulate those, then we'll talk about tomorrow, and I'll prep you for the SWAT training scenarios."

"My top two frustrations, eh?" Rex nodded at my question. "Well, they argued about everything, so narrowing it down won't be easy. I guess the two biggest arguments were around little details and wording."

"Tell me more," Rex prompted.

I explained to him the heated exchange between Seth and Rachel about the sequence in which the customer service reps completed a call with a customer. Then I shared the argument between Seth and Evan about what the inventory system was to be called. He listened intently, asking questions where appropriate.

"I can sum up your problems with one phrase," Rex diagnosed after I was done sharing the day's frustrations. "Consistent where critical; variable where valued."

"Has a nice ring to it, but what does it mean?"

"It means you and your team are getting too hung up on little things which don't really matter, like the order of the processes. It also means you're not getting hung up enough on the important things which do matter, like effective communication."

"Why should we waste our time on wording?" I asked.

"In police work, terminology can make or break the success of an entry. Tomorrow when we are planning our entrances in the stronghold, you'll see us draw a map of the house." Rex grabbed a napkin and created a quick example for me:

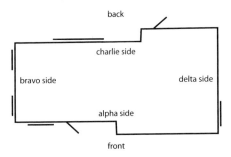

"Have you ever seen a house or a building and never been sure about which side was really the front?" I thought about his question and nodded. Rex continued, "If we used terms like front, back, or side it could cause confusion when it came time to enter the stronghold. We have a whole set of terms we use to make sure we're on the same page. Remember, 'consistent where critical.' If you have inconsistent inputs into your system—in this case, the terminology used—the outputs from your system can get really messed up. In this example, a misstep in terminology means I could have operators entering the stronghold from the wrong side. We know the side of the stronghold facing the street is the 'alpha' side, then we just work our way clockwise around the stronghold. Virtually any SWAT operator around the nation knows what the alpha side of a stronghold is. Similarly, the entrance we go through has to be consistent as well. We number the possible entrances on each side, doors and windows, left to right, bottom to top." He drew on another napkin.

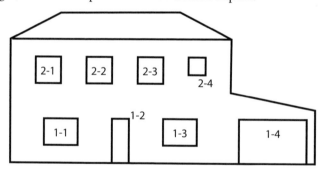

alpha side

"So in my case, Evan was right when he said terminology was a big deal for the Inventory Control System."

"It would appear so, yes. For the other issue, you're dealing with the process rather than an input. The same result will occur regardless of which order things are done. Although, I think I'd agree with Seth's assessment of the situation. That's why we

talk about 'variable where valued.' As SWAT operators, there are many things which are non-negotiable in our jobs to keep us alive and protected. However, we have to be alert and use our heads because sometimes we have to deviate when it makes sense."

"How can you tell the difference between what's gotta be consistent and what can be varied?" I challenged Rex only because it seemed too simplistic.

"Fair question. The answer is in your output, your accomplishment. Ask yourself whether what you're doing will support the output if it's done the same way over and over again. Then figure out if there is any wiggle room allowed. Remember, these aren't polar opposites; consistent and variable are points on a continuum. You just have to figure out where your process falls on the line between the two extremes. In police work, we tend to err on the side of consistency. In your business, I would think dealing with customers would require a little more variability."

"OK, I think I get it." To prove it, and to Rex's amusement, I pulled out the notebook and wrote:

S.W.A.T. FLYER

Consistent where
Critical.

Variable where
Valued.

"It'll make more sense tomorrow when you see the team in action," Rex assured me.

That was an understatement.

Chapter 4

"For the things we have to learn before we can do them, we learn by doing them."

-Aristotle

One of the distinctive traits of a Midwest summer is you get to enjoy both excruciating heat and oppresive humidity. This morning, as I headed to the address Rex provided me for the SWAT training, it was shaping up to be a typical day.

As Rex had mentioned earlier, the training was being held at an abandoned farm house which was about to be demolished. Housing developments had sprung up all around the house, and when the previous home owners passed away and their children could not find an individual buyer, the developers bought the property. Occasionally the SWAT commanders are made aware of these opportunities, and they provide excellent training grounds for the teams, who can beat the heck out of the house before it is leveled.

I found a parking spot on the yard at the end of a long line of squad cars. There was a lot of hustling as the guys on Rex's team were huddled around their van gearing up. Each SWAT operator was putting on what looked like an uncomfortable amount of gear and equipment. Rex had explained to me the purpose of the uniform was to protect the operator, regardless of climate. Just looking at them in their long-sleeves, long pants, helmets, boots, protective vests, padding, and gloves made me uncomfortable on their behalf. They were going to roast, but since this was part of their training, they were probably better prepared for it than I would have been if I were in their place.

Rex's team encompassed police tactical members from multiple suburbs. Each suburban team could act independently or in conjunction with other departments as needs arose. For today, each team was going to be practicing scenarios separately, with one final scenario which would require everybody to work together.

Rex made some opening comments to the teams, including introducing me as an observer. The reactions from the operators were mixed, ranging from a pleasantly welcoming acknowledgment to a scowl at the outside intrusion. That really didn't faze me, especially after dealing with the cold reception I'd received from my own team at SysteMuscle. After he completed his remarks, Rex handed me a bright fluorescent vest, telling me if I wanted to observe anything from inside the stronghold, the vest would identify me as being "out of play."

"I doubt you want these guys tackling you, Toby." Rex explained that the "bad guys" for the day were other police officers who had volunteered to serve as role players for the various scenarios.

I followed Rex to the debrief area for the first scenario of the day. There was a whiteboard posted on the outside of the team's equipment trailer. Rex drew an overhead view of the house and the garage, similar to what he had shown me the day prior.

"Blue Team," Rex addressed the group of men, all of whom were listening intently. "We're going to serve a drug warrant. We know there are, at a minimum, two people in the stronghold, but we suspect there may be as many as four individuals. Your team will stack on the Charlie side of the garage—here ..." he pointed to the back of the garage with his laser pointer,

"... which'll position you to make an entrance into Bravo one-two of the stronghold. No negotiator was used in this scenario, and the dispatcher has informed us at least one individual may be in danger if the element of surprise is compromised."

I followed the team and watched as they lined up behind the garage, just as Rex had directed. It was then I noticed something interesting: The foot position of each of the operators was exactly the same. Each of the men had his right foot forward and his left foot back. They appeared to advance in almost lock step as they moved stealthily from the garage to the house. I watched in awe as they coordinated their movement almost seamlessly. This must have been one of the things Rex meant when he talked about "consistent where critical."

"Police! Open up! We have a warrant!" yelled the team leader. There was no answer from the house. He repeated his command, testing the door knob. It was locked from the inside, so he motioned the operator with the battering ram to come forward. With one quick motion, he knocked open the door, and I watched the entire team proceed into the house. Since I hadn't started inside the house, Rex asked me to continue to watch from the outside, so I had to rely on what I could see through the windows and what I could hear from a distance. There was a lot of shouting and a lot of footsteps echoing throughout the house. A couple of times, I heard somebody shout "need a man" and eventually, I heard somebody yell out "Dominate!" This word was repeated about five or six times. I heard somebody order a secondary sweep and heard more shuffling around through the old house. Finally, I saw the operators escorting the role players out of the house, their hands cuffed and behind their backs.

Rex introduced me to his entry team leader, a stocky guy with a shaved head and a wide smile. "Sergeant Bic Torbin, meet my cousin, Toby." Bic shook my hand with enthusiasm, but still managed to leave my arm in its socket. Then Rex and Bic turned and talked with the rest of the team, debriefing on what went right and what went wrong during the scenario.

"I'm not sure Bravo One-Two was our best entrance, given where the role players were located," one of the men offered, but he conceded, "but hindsight is always twenty-twenty. The bad guys are never located conveniently enough for us."

"Was there another entrance which might have worked better?" Rex coaxed the young operator to explore his suggestion a little further.

"Charlie One-Three would've been out … led us right to the basement. Everyone was clustered toward the front of the house, so Alpha One-Two might not've worked either. Could we have breached a window?"

"I'm going to have Mack give you all a refresher on breaching over the lunch break, then we'll practice it this afternoon. Given everything we just talked about, Tadd, do you now agree Bravo One-Two was the optimal entry point?"

"I suppose so," Tadd concluded.

The team completed debriefing while the second team was practicing the same exercise Rex's team had just gone through. Rex encouraged them to get some rest and hit the water coolers in the shade with a firm admonishment: "I don't want any heat-related injuries today, got it?"

He motioned for me to walk the perimeter with him and asked if I had any questions. Did I ever!

"Earlier, you mentioned something called a 'stack.' What's that?"

"Did you notice how the team's feet were all in perfect alignment and how their advancement was almost perfectly choreographed?" I nodded. Rex was obviously proud of the way his men performed during the exercise. "The line of the men is called a stack. Part of what makes a successful stack is how well they move together. If they're aligned well—foot position, coordinated movement—that's a good stack."

"Well, your team appeared to stack very well," I commended. "While they were inside, I heard them yell, 'Need a man' a few times. Why?"

"No SWAT operator should ever enter a room by himself. He should always have a man watching his back as he advances. As the stack enters the house, they begin to split up room by room. But until a room is secured, there should never be just one operator there. Did you hear the men yelling 'Dominate!' toward the end?"

"Yeah, what was that about?"

"'Dominate' meant they had successfully secured each room in the house. We let each other know the stronghold is secure by yelling 'Dominate!' Remember our conversation last night about terminology? These types of things fall into the 'consistent where critical' category. I'm guessing by the look on your face you've been starting to think about which of your own processes will be critically consistent."

"Sort of," I admitted, halfheartedly. I was enjoying this experience a lot, and thinking about what I was enduring back at SysteMuscle wasn't as appealing as watching this. "Getting to Tadd's question, how do you decide what's the best entry point?"

"Good question. I think of the stronghold as the environment in which our system operates, so the entry point into the system is important. If we choose the wrong place to enter the stronghold, it can cost the lives of team members ... or those of innocent people being held inside. I let Tadd work through the issue on his own, rather than giving him the right answer. Sometimes we get lucky, but other times we can be as surprised as the people we're trying to apprehend."

"Yeah, I would guess you'd want the element of surprise on your side," I ventured.

"Which leads me to this," Rex said, reaching around behind him and rummaging through his bag. While he was searching, he asked, "Do you know what a flash bang is?"

"Um ... how exhibitionists procreate?" Rex ignored my attempt at humor and produced a small cylindrical device which resembled a modern-looking hand grenade.

"This is how we maintain the element of surprise. Throw

one of these into a room, and it produces two opposite, yet coordinating effects. First, it disorients those in the room when it produces a very bright light as well as a concussion-producing sound. Second, it gets their attention long enough for us to enter without being noticed. In systems thinking, you have to consider both the inputs which come into your process, as well as HOW they're introduced into your process. Some of your inputs need to be eased in, like a new employee who is learning the ropes. Other inputs need to be tossed in and create a lot of noise. My guess is what you're doing now is the equivalent of a flash bang to the four people you're working with."

"That's for sure," I thought about the negative exchanges already with so few encounters under our belt. But I was also starting to get an idea of where we needed to go, based on my observations here. "I'm just not sure how I'm going to get these people to see change is in their best interest. And I'm not sure how I'm going to get them to let go of the past in order to move on."

We wrapped up our quick conversation, and Rex asked if I'd like to see the last team go through the scenario from the inside. He made sure I was equipped with both eye and ear protection, and he cautioned me to stay out of the way by staying near a wall or in a corner. We went into the house while the role players were setting back up. We found a good vantage point for me to watch the action by the wall opposite the entry door. Miraculously, the door was still relatively intact despite being beat up by the first two teams.

Through one of the windows, I watched the Orange Team—each team was color coded for easier identification—advance from behind the garage. The role players had to pretend they didn't know they were coming, which had to be difficult the third time around. One of the five role players had a last minute idea, and went into the little half-bathroom near the entrance, giving me a "let's see if they figure this out" grin before he went in.

"Police! Open Up! We have a warrant!" came the warning shout from the entry team leader. A second later, a sea of camouflaged SWAT operators came pouring through the door, which had now been knocked off its hinges after numerous dates with the battering ram. As Rex had indicated, they split up in pairs to search each room, occasionally indicating when they "needed a man" to cover their back side. I watched a SWAT operator walk into the half bathroom. Seeing the role player sitting on the toilet, he was taken aback, apologized for the intrusion and backed out, belying his Midwestern manners. He quickly came to his senses and went back in, dragging the guy out with his pants half-way down his legs. He put him face down on the floor, cuffed him, and frisked him. The SWAT operator looked a little sheepish about hesitating, and he knew he would hear about it later during the debrief. Rex had told me the role players were very good at what they did because of their creativity and their ability to introduce new situations at the last second to keep the SWAT operators alert.

One of the other role players had barricaded himself in a closed room upstairs, and the operators were having a difficult time getting to him without risking potential danger. All of a sudden, I heard somebody shout "ZERO!" followed by a monstrously penetrating explosion from above. Loose plaster dust fell from the ceiling above me, cascading a snow of white powder on everyone still in the rooms on the main floor. I deduced the noise was the infamous flash bang Rex had told me about, and even with the ear protection, I could tell the impact had its desired effect as I heard the scuffle upstairs as the operators brought down the perpetrator.

Finally, the shouts of "Dominate!" came from each of the rooms around the house as the team moved all of the role players—now cuffed—into one central location. While they were being guarded, the team members performed a secondary sweep of the stronghold. This was their quality control check to ensure they hadn't missed anything, or any one, before handing over the crime scene to the detectives for further investigation. At last, they escorted the cuffed role players outside and started their debrief. While he didn't get into trouble, the one operator was ribbed considerably about the bathroom incident.

The next scenario all three teams ran through was a domestic hostage situation. Because the negotiators were not available to participate, the team made the assumption negotiations had broken down and it was imperative for the team to make their entry. Again, I was able to watch from different vantage points, and "consistent where critical, variable where valued" came into much clearer focus as each team performed certain elements routinely, yet maintained some wiggle room for the unknown variables the role players introduced. One such incident occurred when the perpetrator forced his hostage onto the porch roof out of a second story window. The team had to figure out how to apprehend the criminal without hurting the victim. It took some last minute creativity, but they were able to pull it off.

After all three teams had finished this scenario, it was time for lunch. Rex informed all three teams there would be a demonstration on breaching a window before the next role play took place. He instructed them where to reconvene and when. Then he and Bic and I all headed off to eat under a shade tree.

As we were eating, it became apparent Rex's fascination with accomplishment and systems thinking was finding its way through the team. Both Rex and Bic discussed the morning's activities in terms of the outputs achieved and the inputs which created them. I listened intently as the two shared the feedback loops they were using to measure the effectiveness of the outputs: the time it took from entry until exit; the number of glitches identified; any communication breakdowns; and simulated injuries to the role players or the SWAT operators. These two knew their stuff ... but what was disturbing to my ego was it seemed they knew my stuff as well.

I asked Bic how Rex had pulled him on board with the systems thinking stuff. He and Rex just laughed at the question. When Bic sobered, he asked if I'd like to ride along with him sometime when he was on patrol. I looked at Rex as if to ask permission, and he nodded. I ride along with Rex at least once every couple of months. Generally, they're uneventful, with the exception of a speeding ticket or two, but it gives us a chance to get caught up. It almost felt weird accepting an invitation from another cop, but obviously Rex had his reasons for encouraging me to go with Bic, so I accepted. We agreed to touch base sometime later the following week to find a time and date which would work well for us.

The lunch break conversation seemed to fly by more quickly than I would've liked, but I was curious about the breaching demonstration. I knew from watching and listening that breaching was just another word for forcing entry into the stronghold. We all met in the front room of the house, which had most likely served as a living room or sitting room when the house was in its prime.

Senior Officer Mack Marinaro picked up a tool which looked like it meant business from either end, and he asked the crowd in front of him if they knew what it was. Many yelled out it was a "hallagan tool, for breaking and raking." Mack acknowledged their answer, handed the tool to a sufficiently padded officer and sent him outside.

"The trick to breaching," Mack began, "is to get a clean break and make sure you rake the glass fragments so a clear entry can occur without injury." Mack motioned for everybody to back away so they were clear of the window. When he felt everybody was outside of range, he motioned to the SWAT operator outside.

CRASH! The window shattered into hundreds of shards. Then the operator took the other end of the tool and quickly and efficiently raked the glass from all four sides of the pane until the opening was sufficiently smooth. Then he entered through the window himself, and bowed to the applause of his teammates.

The demonstration was effective, and many of the operators went up and examined the window. The next training scenario was going to involve a breach, so everybody prepared to execute the objective. I held back, asking Rex if I could stay inside and watch the breaching exercises. He cautioned me to keep my eyes open and be very careful to stay away from the entry point. I promised I would.

The first team approached the house from the Alpha Side, breaking the ground floor window remaining after the earlier demonstration. They were able to enter without much difficulty, secure the stronghold, and exit through the side door which had been used during the first scenario.

The second team approached from the Delta Side, which up to this point had remained relatively undamaged. There was a large bump-out with a bay-style window. Because the main floor was raised, the operators had to use a small step ladder in order to effectively breach the window. They breached the lower pane and two operators successfully entered. As the third operator—young, inquisitive Tadd—was starting through the window, I noticed the upper pane had jarred loose and was teetering precariously over the operator. I had promised Rex I wouldn't interfere, but this looked bad if it came loose. The first operator was standing close to me, and I tapped him on the shoulder to get his attention and pointed at the upper frame. He reacted quickly, pulling Tadd through the window and motioning the fourth operator back to prevent him from coming through. The moment Tadd was pulled through, the pane shook loose and came crashing straight down, landing outside the window. The others then came through without incident, and they proceeded to secure the stronghold as the first team had. Nobody mentioned the window pane incident, which was fine with me.

The third team attempted to breach a sliding door on the Bravo Side of the house. What they didn't anticipate was the sliding doors were made from shatter-proof reinforced glass. After multiple attempts to break the glass, the team made a decision to change to the Charlie Side and successfully attacked one of the windows in the back of the house. Entry occurred, and the stronghold was secured as with the two prior teams. Then it hit me. The processes at SysteMuscle were like the sliding door. If we were to "dominate" our processes, we needed to successfully breach the old processes in order to make things work for the future.

S.W.A.T. FLYER

If you can't breach the old processes, then we won't be able to dominate the new processes.

The final exercise of the day involved a situation in which one of the role players pretended to be a military explosives expert who had gone off-his-rocker and was holding his family hostage. They combined the three teams into a single integrated entry strategy. The scenario included certain traps set off by the entry teams which would release smoke bombs. The teams would then see there was a different environment and need to make a course correction; namely, they would need to put on their gas masks. I watched from the outside as they teams entered from different sides of the house. When they began breaching the stronghold, they triggered a series of minor explosive traps which generated billows of smoke. The operators then quickly put on their gas masks, found the perpetrator and his hostages inside the house, and finally secured the stronghold. I stood close enough to the house to hear a lot of the action. At the beginning, chaos reigned, but as soon as the operators put on their gas masks and used their flashlights, they were able to achieve their assigned objective quickly.

This exercise confirmed what I'd been suspecting about my own situation. My team members were being very slow at recognizing their own changing environment. The smoke was there; they just didn't see the fire ... nor did they know how to react to it. Somehow, I needed to get them to understand the sporting goods industry was not the same as it was when SysteMuscle first began. Many rapidly-expanding companies experience growing pains, but those who respond quickly to changes in the environment are usually able to adjust and keep up with their growth. The task at hand was to make sure my team realized what their reality was. And then I came up with an idea that just might work.

S.W.A.T. FLYER

If the system's environment changes, then either the inputs, the transformation, or the outputs will **HAVE TO CHANGE**.

Chapter 5

"The best way out is always through."

-Robert Frost

There is one thing I've learned about cubicle-dwelling, and it's how to build connections with people who really count: receptionists and administrative assistants, security guards and help desk administrators, facilities staff and maintenance custodians. Sucking up to executives and managers does not yield the same results as befriending those who can really help get things done in an organization.

Today, Howard from Facilities Management is my key resource. The guy has an affinity for fine cigars, so I always make sure he's well stocked. Now it's time to call in a favor. Since we know where our meeting rooms will be for the duration of this project, I've devised a little plan to help "motivate" my team to see the need for change.

"OK, Howard, you know what I need and when?"

"Right-O, Tobe-ster. Don't worry about it. They won't know what hit 'em."

"You're the best!" I really do mean the compliment. The man has helped me out in so many ways, especially since Rona continues to throw roadblocks in front of me. Howard is my default work-around solution … I think of him as MacGyver's brain in Homer Simpson's body.

My own brain has been racing at high speed since watching the SWAT training. The last meeting with the team had me stumped on how to convey the importance of changing our processes, even though our company appears to be doing well enough in the sporting goods distribution industry. All of the great change gurus say you have to make the pain of the status quo high enough or people will never change. My team hasn't seen any pain yet, since all they look at are the internal company figures.

I've been observing them since we started meeting, and one behavioral trait struck me at our last meeting: They're all coffee drinkers. I don't mean sip-a-mug-here-and-there coffee drinkers; they are bring-a-thermos-and-settle-down-for-the-long-haul coffee drinkers. If they could take it intravenously, they would. I'm counting on this to be their downfall.

The team filed into the room right on time (they're punctual if nothing else). I posted the agenda on the wall for this meeting, listing the next series of current-state processes for us to document. It was pretty aggressive for us to try to get through ten processes in a half day, but all of them were relatively small ones without a lot of variations, so with some concerted effort, I knew we could pull it off.

I began the meeting by sharing my earlier conversation with Rona. Rachel scoffed. Evan rolled his eyes. Elena looked surprised. Seth's expression was blank. This news immediately created another argument about the futility of our assignment.

"I've said it before," ramped up Rachel, "our industry isn't doing that bad. We're still beating many of our competitors in this market. Most of the established names still use us as a distributor because we've been around a while. We're just wasting our time here."

"What about some of the newer brands launched in the past couple of years?" I challenged.

"Doesn't matter," Seth interrupted. "I still say if we'd just use a Six Sigma or Lean methodology, we'd be done by now." He took a long sip of coffee, and his face got a funny look as he loosened his collar a little. "Say, is it getting warm in here?"

"Nah," I replied nonchalantly. "Must be your imagination."

Evan interjected, "We've covered this with you in every meeting so far: We know how to do our jobs. You don't." He turned to Seth, pushing his own coffee mug away, "Now that you mention it, it does seem a little warm in here."

"Bad coffee?" I asked with as much innocence as I could muster.

"There's another thing you don't know," Evan retorted. "There's no such thing as bad coffee. Only bad coffee makers."

"Still none of you seem to be interested in drinking it."

"It's kind of hard to enjoy the morning coffee when the room is so blasted hot," Evan shot back. "Don't you feel it, or are you dense on basic temperature interpretation as well?"

"Feel what? The room feels the same as it always has." I walked to the cooler I'd stashed at the end of the table and pulled out a cold bottle of water. As I opened it up and started to drink, four sets of eyes rested upon me, deciding whether they should just be envious, or go all the way, mug me and steal my water.

"What?" My acting skills were improving.

"Did you bring enough for everybody?" Rachel asked in a mocking voice.

"But I thought coffee was the only drink for you." My response matched her mocking tone syllable for syllable. "Could it be the environment has changed a little? Is it possible what was good enough for you last week isn't working now?"

"What are you talking about?" Evan was getting irritable, as he loosened his collar some more.

"I get it, and I think it's a brilliant analysis." This time, I joined in the shock. The response came from Elena. She continued her explanation directed at the others. "Toby understands our business is changing. And it is changing, whether we admit it or not. What he's done is make us all see that when the environment changes, in this case our room temperature, the way we have done business in the past— drinking coffee—no longer works."

"Excellent! You got it!" I summarized as I tossed her a cold one. Elena smiled at the gesture.

The others were torn between being in awe that Elena actually said something and being annoyed with me for pulling off this object lesson. I walked to the conference room phone and called Howard.

"Mission accomplished," I spoke into the receiver. "You can put the conference room temp back to normal." Howard affirmed my request, and within a minute, cool air was again shooting out of the vents in the conference room. I took the opportunity to jot a note in my book:

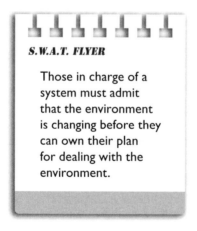

S.W.A.T. FLYER

Those in charge of a system must admit that the environment is changing before they can own their plan for dealing with the environment.

"OK, OK, you made your point," sighed Seth, exasperated. "Things are changing in our industry … maybe more than any of us want to admit. Still, tossing us into the fiery furnace was a bit much, wasn't it?"

"I still don't think things are changing so terribly much," huffed Rachel.

"You don't have to deal with the same customer complaints I do, Rachel," Evan came to my defense. "Keep in mind, my team is the one handling it when the rest of you screw up." This comment elicited another round of shouting and arguing, and it took a few minutes to calm everyone down again. I then tried to refocus their attention to the current state process flows. Because there was marginally more buy-in from the team, the pace picked up a little as we worked on charting out each process.

By the end of the half-day meeting, we had completed the ten processes I had identified as well as an additional four I had on slate for the next meeting. Even Elena was engaged now, and she began sharing some of the technical aspects of what happens behind the scenes in the Call Center. The momentum was amazing.

We continued meeting throughout the week. The only major hitches we encountered were when the words "yeah, but what if …" started the sentence. Then we knew we would have to document some kind of decision diamond in the process and branch out into more than one path on the process flow. This is where Seth's knowledge of each and every management and information technology fad made itself useful. He explained one type of process mapping called a "use case," where people would make note of the "happy path." This was the most commonly followed path through the process; the one where everything goes right. We still documented the other paths through the process, but made sure we noted which one was most commonly followed and which ones were the result of "yeah, but what if." By tracking the happy path, we could more easily see what inputs (decisions) were leading to what outputs (other processes).

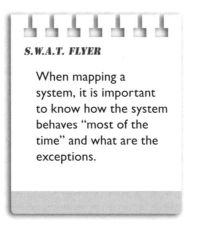

S.W.A.T. FLYER

When mapping a system, it is important to know how the system behaves "most of the time" and what are the exceptions.

The other area which seemed to slow the team down was whenever the players they were documenting had to interact with a phone system, computer system, or paper trail. For these, we started making notes below the bottom lane to document where these interactions took place.

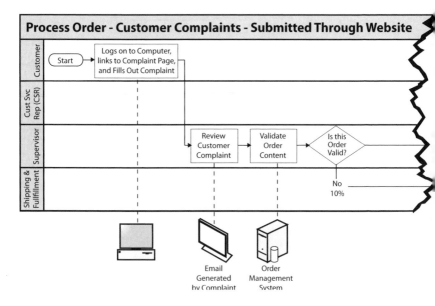

Process Order - Customer Complaints - Submitted Through Website

Some processes were repetitive and simple, and we were able to assign them to individual team members to take back to their desks and work on outside of the team meetings. Then we discussed and approved them at the beginning of the following meeting. Within just a couple of weeks of having started, we had completed almost all of the current state processes, and they were looking pretty solid.

The team asked for a couple of days off to review the current state process flow charts and to share them with their teams before we continued. This break would also allow us to get caught up on some of the other work piling up on our desks during all of the half-day meetings. I was glad to get back to my desk as well. In addition to facilitating the team, Rona had not let up on any of my other duties; in fact, she was being more demanding than ever. At least now we had the first step—the current "as is" processes—complete with a little less than a month to define our desired accomplishments and document the new processes which would get us there. I knew this next step was not going to be easy,

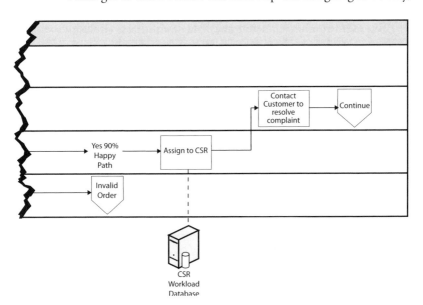

however. There was a lot of territorialism at SysteMuscle, even within departments. Because of the culture Doug and Rona had created, many managers had grown possessive of their turf, and this mind-set had trickled down to supervisors and employees.

At least the team had been cooperative for the past week. I wasn't sure what had gotten into Elena, but she was an amazingly valuable member to the team, and her participation shifted the dynamics. Her handling of Rachel, Evan, and Seth was fascinating. Whenever one of them began to get out of line, Elena would simply make a soft comment answering the question at hand. Sometimes she'd just look at them, raise her eyebrow, and smile, and the bickering stopped. I was perplexed about what prompted her to start participating. She was still soft-spoken, and I found myself wishing she would more actively engage the rest of the team rather than just react to their squabbles. This was at least a move in the right direction.

During our break, I thought it would be prudent to give Rona a status update, so she knew where we were. I also hoped it would build a little more confidence in me. Silly me.

"You mean you haven't defined a single new process?" Rona drawled somewhat condescendingly. "This is disappointing, even for you." The implication was obvious and made me bristle.

"Maybe if you took the time to understand business processes instead of just passing judgment, you might be able to comprehend what we're doing," I attempted to match her level of condescension.

"Now, let's not be a little man about this." Who was she kidding? Did she think I was a four-year-old? "I guess I'll just have to tell Doug the team is still progressing slowly … primarily because of you."

I gave her my trademark shrug. "Whatever you want, Rona. I have real work to do." I wasn't about to wait to be excused from her highness's office, and I wasn't going to waste time engaging her in a losing battle.

That night at dinner, my wife Molly and I were both

unusually quiet. Normally, we were very conversational while making supper. For the first couple of hours after we got home, we'd typically chat and laugh about the day. While we didn't always agree on everything, we were in sync on what really mattered. However, tonight, I was too self-absorbed to notice her quietness, but she was too perceptive to ignore mine. We went through the motions of eating dinner, and by the time she brought out dessert, she finally ventured to ask the obvious question, "Is everything OK?"

"May I quit my job?" I blurted out in response to her question.

"Quit … your … job … ?" Molly repeated slowly.

"I have to get away from SysteMuscle." The words just started gushing out and I explained everything going on the last three weeks with Rona and the team and trying to get them to understand systems thinking and process flows and how we were making headway but it wasn't good enough for Rona. I stood up and started pacing around the room as sentences and sentiments tumbled over each other in an emotional plea to obtain her permission to let me look for another job. Molly had been the only reason I'd stayed after Rona's rise to power. Generally resistant to change, Molly had watched her family suffer when her dad was downsized from his corporate job during her childhood. They almost had to file for bankruptcy, and she was very protective of a secure income. But I could tell something else was bothering Molly about my request, and it had nothing to do with her own concerns about financial security, at least not directly.

"Toby, sit down," she requested. Uh-oh. Nothing good ever started with a request to sit down. "Honey, I know you are miserable at your job, and I really respect the sacrifice you go through to stick it out there, especially since Doug stepped away. But we have another reason to have you stay there."

There was a long pause as the impact of her words sunk in.

"What now?" I sighed.

"I got the call today from the university. I've been accepted into the doctoral program. This is something I've always wanted, and it will position me well for what I really want to do with my life. Your employer at least helps with tuition reimbursement for spouses. While SysteMuscle may not be the best place to work, their benefits are very generous. Without that assistance, there's no way I can do this program. I've worked so hard to get in. I didn't want to say anything until I knew for sure I'd be accepted." Molly's eyes filled up with tears.

I wasn't really sure how to react to this news. I hugged Molly and assured her I would get things worked out. Inside, I was feeling a little resentful toward my wife and the situation. It was her insecurity and her goals which had effectively held me hostage at a job I hated the past couple of years. Now she was asking me to continue with it even though things had become progressively worse. Love and resentment are incompatible inputs into the emotional system. I knew I'd have to deal with it at some point, but now was probably not the time.

A couple of days later, the team reunited to start going through all of the suggestions and changes they'd gathered for the current state "as is" process flowcharts. There weren't many, but each change seemed to generate significant discussion. By the time we had covered all of the proposed changes, there was less than an hour left to our meeting. I started to share my strategy for defining the future state "to be" processes. The two day break had not been good for their behavior, as they reverted back to their old ways.

"Do we really need to change so much?" Rachel challenged. "There's nothing really wrong with how we do things that a little tweaking won't solve."

I thought back to the SWAT observation and the breaching demonstration. I knew if we were really going to make a clean entry into a new way of doing things, we were going to have to "break and rake" the old ways. They would make a good frame of reference, and certainly some of them might stay the same if there was a good business reason not to change. My problem was explaining those reasons to this team without going into all of the detail about SWAT teams and breaking glass and flash bang devices.

"At our meeting tomorrow, let's start talking about what outputs we want and what inputs we need to make a customer order work, OK?

With the exception of Elena, there was the requisite grumbling and muttering from the other three as they left the room. Again, I was feeling defeated. Again, Rex must have been sensing my frustration, since his e-mail was the first to pop into my in-box.

FROM: Lt. Rex Donovan
TO: Toby Donovan
SUBJECT: Systems Thinking Object Lesson
DATE: 4 August

Toby:

The guys enjoyed meeting you the other day. I heard you saved Tadd from an unnecessary "shave"—we'll make a cop out of you yet. I have a surprise for you. Come by the police station tonight after supper … say around 8-ish. I'll meet you at the front entrance.

Props
Rex

Now what could he be up to?

SWAT – Seize the Accomplishment

Chapter 6

"It is a capital mistake to theorize before one has data."

-Arthur Conan Doyle

Rex met me at the door of the police station and threw a visitor's badge around my neck from fifteen feet away. When we were children, he was the ring-toss king of the family, and it was obvious he hadn't lost his touch. We wound through the maze of offices and cubicles. A couple of the SWAT team guys who were on break from their patrol duties, recognized me, and waved their greetings from across the break room.

Rex escorted me out the back door of the police station across a parking lot to a nondescript brick and concrete building, about 50 yards long and yet only about ten yards wide. Rex went through the requisite security ritual to gain access to the building. He still wasn't telling me why he had invited me here, or what we were doing, but I always knew with Rex there was an adventure in store, and I resigned myself long ago to just go with the flow where my cousin was concerned.

"OK, so what's going on?" I decided to just ask rather than have another surprise sprung on me.

"Your first shooting lesson." Rex didn't bat an eye.

"My first WHAT?" I couldn't believe my ears. "Rex, you

know how I feel about guns and stuff. My wife and my mom would both shoot me if they knew where I was."

Rex gave an amused chuckle at the irony of my comment. Then he proceeded to head to the gun cabinet and pull out a couple of handguns. Without even saying a word, his body language gave me the disapproving look of "Get over it, ya big sissy. You're going to learn to shoot a gun today, whether you want to or not."

What Rex actually said was, "Toby, I watched you at the last scenario training. Your eyes were fixed on those guns. There were a couple of minutes I thought I was going to have to tie a drool bib on you. Say what you want, but I think you actually want to learn to do this."

I couldn't argue with his logic. I'd been brainwashed in a way. My mom put the fear of guns into me from an early age. As an insurance claims examiner, she used to pay NRA claims, and I heard every "stupid hunter" story imaginable. My wife was completely averse to firearms; she had never held a gun, and she had no interest in ever handling one. I believe her exact words on the subject were "handguns are dangerous and pointless."

"OK," I mumbled against my better judgment. "I'll give it a shot … no pun intended."

"Great," said Rex, handing me a Glock 17 nine millimeter handgun. "This is the easiest handgun to shoot. It's empty right now, because I want to cover a few safety lessons before I let you actually fire at anything."

He then proceeded to cover a lot of issues regarding handgun safety. He made sure I had eye and ear protection. We talked about the importance of stance and how to hold a gun, both when in use and when at rest. He emphasized a gun should never be pointed at anybody unless I was planning on actually shooting them. These directives meant the gun should either remain at my side, pointed to the ground in front of me, or in my holster, depending on the situation. Basically, the gun should be pointed in whichever direction is the safest. Then Rex asked me to do something I wasn't expecting.

"Breathe," he commanded suddenly.

"Breathe?" I asked, as though seeking clarification.

"Yes, breathe. You know … inhale, exhale, inhale, exhale … that whole thing."

"Yeah, I got it … actually, I've been pretty good at it since birth, which is how I got this far. Any reason why you want me to demonstrate the skill now?"

"As a matter of fact, yes. I want you to hold the gun with your shooting hand, and support it with your non-shooting hand, as I showed you." I complied. "Now point it over at that red brick on the wall." (Again, I followed orders obediently.) "Now close your eyes and take some deep breaths."

I inhaled, filling up my lungs with air and my nostrils with the industrial mustiness of the indoor shooting range. Slowly I exhaled. I repeated the process a few more times, never breaking my stance, but eventually I opened my eyes and refocused on the target. When I was in the middle of my next exhale, Rex yelled, "Pull the trigger!"

Instinctively, I reacted and fired. Since the gun was empty, it was a dry fire. I put the gun down at my side and gave Rex a look of "Yeah, so now what?"

"You just fired on what we call the 'half lung.' This is going to sound kind of Zen-like, but your breathing is going to be important in shooting."

"This is a shooting lesson, not Lamaze class. What does breathing have to do with shooting a gun?" I was getting a little impatient at this point, and I really was in no mood for his Sensei-grasshopper approach to firearms.

"How did you feel when you were exhaling?" Rex inquired.

"I dunno … relaxed, I guess."

"Exactly! Tension is the last thing you need when firing a gun. Being put in the position of firing a gun is tense enough. Regulating your breathing is just one of the ways to maintain control of the many variables you have to consider when firing your weapon. We teach our SWAT counter-snipers to fire when they have completely exhaled—or on an empty lung as we call it—just because of the heightened focus and the ability required. While not every department agrees with this philosophy, we do all agree on one thing: Breathing is a critical component to hitting your target.

It seemed to make sense. Rex could tell I was processing this information. He held out his hand and gestured for me to hand him the gun. He took it, set it down on the table, and walked over to a storage cabinet to the side of the shooting range where we were standing. He pulled out a large sheet of paper and came back to fasten it to the target. On the poster-sized sheet was a mean-looking muscular male with a really bad mullet. He was holding a gun in his left hand, and it was pointed directly at me. Superimposed on the picture was a pattern of squares and numbers. Rex explained the area around his chest and his head was referred to as the "lethal zone." A shot to one of these areas was fatal.

"Well, with the bad hair, I suppose it's only fair to put him out of his misery," I mused. Rex smiled at the comment.

He walked back to the table where the weapon was lying. He popped out the magazine and loaded one bullet. Replacing the magazine into the gun, he carefully handed it back, handle toward me, barrel pointed to the ground.

"Now, I want you to practice the stance we discussed." After I was comfortable with my stance, Rex helped me align the gun's barrel with the target, as he had shown me earlier. Finally, he encouraged me to think about my breathing. I stood there, contemplating my target, and pulling together all of the directions he had given me. Then I pulled the trigger. There was surprisingly little kick-back from the gun. I looked at the target poster and saw I grazed the edge of the poster.

"Not bad," Rex said.

"I missed," came my reply, rather matter-of-factly.

"But …?" Rex was going somewhere, but I wasn't sure where, so I just shrugged. "You hit the paper … for your first time handling a gun … pretty good." He then stepped up to where the target was hanging and pointed out all of the bullet holes in the ceiling and surrounding wall, making it very clear my aim wasn't the only bad one.

"I'm sure I can do better than those," I stated confidently.

"I'm sure you can, too," he agreed. "There is one other thing to remember, though, and this is important. When you were lining up your shot—stance, line of sight, breathing—you had your finger on the trigger. Big no-no in our world. Never—and I repeat, never—have your finger on the trigger until you're ready to shoot. Too many accidents happen when guys pull the trigger before they mean to. Don't become one of those statistics your mom has scared you about over the years."

"Got it. Finger off the trigger."

He put another single bullet in my gun, and allowed me to practice. This time, I worked at remembering all of the components he had talked about, and I kept my finger off the trigger until it was time to pull it. My second real shot landed on the outer border of the lethal range, but at least now I was inside the desired target.

"Yes! That shot would have been fatal, or at least put the guy in critical condition!" Rex's excitement concerned me a little, but I wrote it off to his profession.

We continued to work on a series of single shots for about the next fifteen to twenty minutes until I was consistently hitting the target at lethal range with a greater degree of accuracy. After a while, Rex loaded my magazine with three bullets and we moved to a fresh target sheet. The nervousness of handling a firearm was dwindling as my confidence grew. I continued to remember all of the gun safety tips Rex had provided earlier. This was becoming enjoyable, which surprised me a little bit.

After working our way through two boxes of bullets and three target posters, I was becoming startlingly adept at hitting the target. Even Rex was surprised at how quickly I was catching on.

"You're doing better than some of our new recruits. You

wouldn't have an interest in becoming a volunteer reserve officer, would you?" I couldn't tell if Rex was serious or not, so I let the question slide with another shrug. From my body language, I figured Rex could surmise the resistance I would get at home.

We wrapped up the lesson by thoroughly cleaning our weapons. Rex showed me how to take the Glock apart and what parts needed the most thorough cleaning.

"A clean gun is a happy gun," he grinned. "Seriously, this is one of the reasons we win more gun battles with bad guys. They don't take time to clean their guns, so they tend to jam and break more often than ours do. It's all about taking care of your system."

After we cleaned, conditioned, and reassembled each of our handguns, Rex asked me to review what I had learned. I took out my notebook and wrote the main points down while I recited them to Rex:

S.W.A.T. FLYER

✔ Stance - find an aggressive stance I'm comfortable with
✔ Grip - Keep my dominant (firing) arm straight, use my other arm to support my firing arm

S.W.A.T. FLYER

✔ Line of sight - using my dominant eye, align the three "dots" on the gun with the target
✔ Breathe - fire on the half-breath, midway through the exhale, to keep me relaxed

S.W.A.T. FLYER

✔ Trigger - keep my finger off the trigger until I'm ready to shoot
✔ Review - look at the shot placement to get feedback for the next shot
✔ Clean the gun when I'm done

S.W.A.T. FLYER

All inputs must be present for a successful shooting experience.

"Remember," Rex said, putting his finger on the last page I wrote, "all of these are important. Your last observation is right: The others all have to be there to make your shooting experience a positive one. The same is true of systems thinking. Your inputs have to coordinate with each other if you want the kind of output you desire. You can't isolate a single input and say it's the most successful factor for shooting a gun. If you do, you'll develop some really bad habits in shooting, and you'll never learn how to do it properly."

Something clicked, and it wasn't the advancing of the handgun magazine. It was my synapses based on what Rex had just said. All of the inputs had to be present at just the right time. They all had to work together. The trigger needed to be pulled at just the right time when all were in alignment. Those aligned inputs were missing from our SysteMuscle processes! Sure, we had all of them there, but they were coming from a dozen different locations, none of which appeared to be cooperating with the others.

"Earth to Toby," Rex was doing his best astronaut space controller voice. "This is mission control, Toby, we appear to have lost transmission. Repeat. We have lost transmission. Please respond. Over."

"Very funny," I chuckled as I tossed the visitor's badge back at him. A perfect toss.

The next day, I taped all the sheets of a full order form packet on the wall, surrounded by sheets of flip chart paper. Every single blank on each form had the end of a string glued to it. When the team arrived, I asked each person to pick a string and tell me where the information came from to fill in the specific blank. At first, they all looked at me like I was nuts. I was becoming accustomed to those looks, and they don't unnerve me as much as they used to.

"Oh, look, our fearless leader has come up with a new plot in his effort to make us fix something which isn't broken," Rachel started the onslaught.

"All he needs now are his scented markers and his colorful sticky notes and we'll be powerless to resist his charms," Evan threw in with an air of disdain.

"Guys, give it a rest."

Once again, I was grateful Elena was on my side, but what surprised me this time was the intensity in her voice and the expression on her face. She wasn't just mad; she was furious. Elena, who sat in silence during our first few meetings. Elena, who has been mild-mannered and cooperative recently. Elena, who was about to kick some cubicle butt.

"You all have some nerve even being employees here, let alone on this team. You claim to be good corporate soldiers, yet I have never seen such a group of cowards in my life," Elena's face was turning a bit red, a mere hint of what was to come.

"You wouldn't know what a good soldier was if I drew you a picture! Seth, you hide behind every new trend and fad you can find. If you spent as much time doing work as you do trying to derail this team, we would be done with this project by now."

"Now, come on, Elena, you can't really ..." Rachel began but was quickly cut off.

"And you!" Elena turned on Rachel and stood over her. "I've

86   *SWAT – Seize the Accomplishment* never seen such a wimpy attempt at passive-aggression in my life. If you don't like change, Rachel, grow a backbone and be honest with us and then take yourself off the team. Toby has made every fair effort to make this project work, and all you can do is criticize him behind his back and go off and tattle to Rona. You disgust me!" Rachel blanched.

"Toby, are you going to let her talk to us this way?" Evan demanded. "I thought you were supposed to be leading this team. What about our code of conduct?"

"Oh, shut up, Evan!" Elena turned and answered before I could. "If you cared about the code of conduct, your behavior would have changed a long time ago. I, for one, want to see where this project can take us. I wish I were the only one who knew about all of our customer systems, because then I wouldn't have to look at any of you meeting after miserable meeting. Unfortunately, I need the rest of you to provide input. So, shut up, stand up, grab a marker, a string, and a piece of tape, because no one's leaving this room until we have this defined!"

You know those instances when you've just been in a Twilight Zone kind of experience and time stands dead still right before the regular action speeds up again? This was it. It was as though Elena had simultaneously slapped the team in the face while dousing them with cold water.

For the next several minutes, they obediently took the strings I had dangling from the forms and began to label the sources of the data used to complete a customer order. Nobody dared to say a word while processing the information on the wall. Finally—progress! After about a half hour, I called a time out, and the team had a chance to look at what we had covered so far. We discovered the information came from multiple sources: the customer, the customer database files, the dealer web interface, the credit database files, the shipping rates "clipboards," the inventory database files, and the credit card and bank interface. Plus, the customer service representative could override any field at his or her discretion.

Once every string was tied to a data source, I asked the team what they saw.

"A waste of good string?" Again, it was Elena who surprised everybody, but this time the reaction was positive. What started as a couple of giggles grew quickly to uproarious laughter until we were all wiping away tears. No apologies needed. No explanations given. The team had just experienced a breakthrough, and we hadn't even really defined what was going on with the system yet. Once we regained our composure, I tried again.

"None of these systems talk to each other," Seth offered. "If our system output, as you call it, is a successful order, we're dealing with a lot of inconsistent inputs which keep us from getting there. We get the customer address based on what they tell us on the phone or through the internet, but it's already stored in our customer database. If they type it wrong or there's a communication snafu between the customer and the representative on the phone, we have trouble."

"There's more," Rachel added. "Some of these systems provide conflicting information. If the credit card interface denies the customer's card, most of the customer service reps just override it with what is on the customer credit file, which can be up to a month old. We've been seeing a growing trend of credit card issues, and a lot of times the card companies are making us eat the cost because we let the transaction go through when we shouldn't have."

"This brings up another good point," I added. "Our timing on these files appears to be off. Some of them are updated in real-time and provide good data. Others can grow stale for weeks before they are updated. We're pulling the trigger before the gun is aimed or ready." My lesson with Rex was still pretty fresh in my mind.

"Toby, can we make a list of all of the problems we see with these interfaces?" Elena was now taking ownership in this process. "If we know what is wrong, we should be able to use it to make it right."

"Good idea, Elena," I stated, chorused by the other members

88

of the team.

Together, we spent the rest of the meeting, noting all of the places where the inputs to processing a customer order didn't line up, where there was incorrect data, where the timing was off, and where the systems contradicted each other. When we were done, we had compiled quite an overwhelming list.

We recapped the meeting, and it was almost a shock to have everybody finally engaged in a common goal. We set the direction for our next meeting, where we would discuss how to solve most of the data issues we had identified.

The others filtered out the room, and Elena was the last to leave.

"OK, what just happened in here?" My curiosity got the better of me, and I wasn't about to let her go without an explanation.

"It looks like they want to play nice now," she answered innocently.

"Elena …" I paused. Did it really matter why she had done what she did? The bottom line is I was now getting the behaviors I wanted from this team, and I figured it could continue. Elena was still looking at me, expecting me to say something more. "Um … how … I mean, why … I guess … well …."

Elena smiled at my attempts to stumble over my request for an explanation. "Toby, I've worked with this group for years, and as you can tell we've pretty much gotten nowhere. So I quit trying. My inputs were a lesson in futility in their system. When you started working with them, I could see things were … well … different, but I didn't want to jump in feet first. I tested things out a little, and when I saw there was benefit to my contributions, I decided it was time I committed myself to the team. You're the one who taught us about system inputs. I was just using it."

"Thanks," I blurted out.

"Don't mention it," she smiled a really true smile for the first time since I had met her. "You're doing a good job, Toby. Keep it up. Oh … and one other thing in the way of an explanation …" Elena paused before leaving the room, "remember the SWAT operator you saved from crashing glass? He might be somebody's husband, and he said I should return the favor and help you out. Some systems are more connected than you think."

Ain't that the truth ....

Chapter 7

"There are two kinds of light – the glow that illuminates, and the glare that obscures."

-James Thurber

After our experience with the customer order, we decided to take a long, hard look at the outputs which were really important to the Call Center for SysteMuscle. We had spent a lot of time documenting all of the processes they currently do for the "as is" state. We were quickly figuring out the future state needed to be—and could be—a lot more streamlined.

Springboarding from our success at the prior meeting, we agreed to meet the next day. Gone was the drama plaguing us the first few weeks. Since the team was seeing success and the big picture, they were beginning to understand how valuable this could be to all of their jobs.

Before jumping into the "to be" processes, we reviewed the list of the "as is" processes to see if there were any which could be combined or were unnecessary. Then we grouped the remaining processes together into logical categories. As Rex had reminded me multiple times by now, the important part of systems thinking was ultimately the accomplishment. To this end, Elena managed to find a copy of the department's original mission statement: "SysteMuscle Call Center exists as the one and only interface our customers could ever want or need."

"Well, that says absolutely nothing," Evan growled. "It must've been drafted by one of the high-priced consultants from the Coasts Doug used to bring in."

"Not so fast, Evan," I cautioned. "Look at this from a different light. If the mission says this department is the 'one and only interface,' what does it say to you?"

"No more back-door politicking with supervisors and dealers?" Evan ventured a guess.

"Exactly! We have to define our processes in such a way so people actually want to do business with you and your staff. We have to make it a pleasure for them to interface with you."

"OK, Toby, it sounds good," cautioned Rachel, "but how do we make it happen?"

"Not meaning to sound like we're ganging up on you again," interjected Seth, "but she's right. It does sound a little pie-in-the-sky."

"I think I get it," Elena added to the conversation. "It goes back to the systems thinking issue again. If we can define what our outputs are going to be—in this case, the mission—then we can back up to the inputs we need. Our last exercise becomes valuable since we already know where those inputs come from." While Elena was talking, I pulled out my trusty notebook and wrote a quick note.

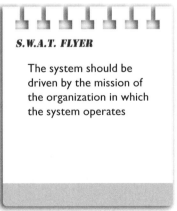

S.W.A.T. FLYER

The system should be driven by the mission of the organization in which the system operates

"Thanks, Elena!" I was truly grateful for her input. "We just need to look at the system in the context of the mission."

"OK, but again, how do we do it?" Seth kept hounding us with this important detail. "This isn't like a game of connect-the-dots where we can just see the relationships. There are so many variables." As much as I hated to admit it, he had a point. Then Evan and Rachel both came to the same conclusion at the same time.

"Define the outputs first!" Everybody laughed at their newfound unity.

"OK, let's define what we want the department to accomplish. We know what your mission says, but what does it mean?" I challenged. "Of all of the things you do, what are the critical outputs which support the mission? From there, what are the processes which require our focus to accomplish those outputs?"

"I suppose those things our customers care about or which help our bottom line," Evan's wisdom in this area was pretty evident, but he still drew some quizzical looks from Rachel and Seth. "I mean, everything boils down to dollars, right? If we're improving our relationships with our customers, it's either going to increase our sales revenue or decrease our cost since we'll be spending less time reacting to our customers when they get bad service."

"So that means we start with effective order-taking," Rachel offered. "After all, if we don't get the order right the first time, what's the point?" I wrote 'effective order taking' on the flip chart.

"What does 'effective' mean?" Elena solicited from the entire team.

"Done right the first time," Evan jumped. "I'm sick and tired of whiny customers who complain about incompetent order-taking."

"In stock," Seth proposed. "After all, one of the biggest reasons we lose orders before we even get them is when we have to tell customers something isn't in stock."

"Yeah, but we can't control that," Rachel argued. "I don't think this should be on the list if we can't control it ourselves."

"But our customers care about it," Seth countered. "Shouldn't it be about their perspective rather than ours?" And before I knew it, Seth and Rachel were escalating into one of their classic debates. However, unlike before, now that we had a fully functioning team, they had become self-policing. Evan and Elena stepped in.

"It's about the outputs, Rachel," Elena suggested. "If an effective order means we have things in stock, then we need to include it."

S.W.A.T. FLYER

The people who care about your outputs are the best source of system feedback you can get.

"Yeah, and I can tell you from experience, inventory issues are one of the key causes of customer complaints," Evan added.

"Whatever," Rachel conceded.

"No 'whatevers,'" Elena challenged her. "We all have to be on board here, or this won't work."

"We still don't have any answers for how we are going to figure out how we'll change these processes just based on knowing inputs and outputs," Rachel continued.

"She has a point," Evan added. "I'm not really comfortable moving forward unless we have a little more of a plan of attack."

"OK, I'll make you a deal … let's sleep on it over the weekend," I conceded. "If I can't provide you with something by

Monday, we'll have to go to Rona and tell her we're stuck."

"Not a pleasant thought," Elena contributed. Everybody just nodded sullenly.

When I arrived back at my desk, I worked through the massive number of e-mails which seemed to plague me since I was spending all of my time in meetings. I managed to sort through the ones that were more informational, highlighted a small number where I needed to take action, deleted the unnecessary ones the spam filter didn't catch, and ignored the annoying forwards from friends and family. There was one in particular which caught my eye.

FROM: Sgt. Bic Torbin
TO: Toby Donovan
SUBJECT: Ride Along?
DATE: 14 August

Toby:

You wouldn't have any interest in riding along with me tonight on patrol, would you? Rex thought it might be beneficial for you to get away from it all and see how the other half lives.

Call to confirm. You already have my number.

Peace out, buddy!
Bic

Once again, I found myself showing up at the police station at an unexpected hour. I managed to catch a power nap after work. While I had a long list of to-do's piling up at home, I felt compelled to take up Bic on his offer. He met me at the back door with his trademark big cheesy grin.

"Rex owes me twenty," he joked. "He didn't think I'd be able to lure you into a night shift ride along on short notice."

"I want a cut of the bounty," I grumped. I didn't like giving up sleep. I needed all I could get. The stress of meeting the deadline while dealing with Rona was starting to get to me, and I could feel it. Rex was noticing a change in me as well, because he was increasingly hounding me about my health, fitness, and diet. He reminded me systems thinking also applied to over-all health and well-being. Personally, I found it annoying, even if I agreed with him.

Bic just laughed at my reference, as he handed me a visitor's badge and gave me the requisite liability release paperwork to sign. I had never been on a police patrol "ride along" with anyone but Rex before, but after all I had been through so far, my intuition was telling me both Bic and Rex had an ulterior motive for this particular invitation. Why they selected the third watch was beyond me, though.

"Come on in, we're about to start roll call," Bic invited. Bic was the shift Sergeant, but he often patrolled right along with his team. We met with the handful of officers who were on night patrol, some of whom I recognized from the SWAT observation of a few days—or was it now weeks?—prior. The third watch for this department ran from 11:00 PM until 7:00 AM. While I had become quite a night owl with the long hours I had been putting in for this project, I hadn't pulled an "all-nighter" since my college days, and to be honest I wasn't sure I still had it in me.

Roll call was a brief meeting with the patrol officers on shift. Bic led the meeting, scrolling through some of the recent incident reports from the dispatchers. It seemed fairly routine—a couple of domestic abuses, some shoplifters, a few notable traffic violations. What amused me was the color commentary from Bic and the other guys. They all seemed to maintain a healthy sense of humor about many of the cases discussed.

After Bic sent his staff out, we headed to his car. He made the obligatory safety check of his patrol car, ensuring all of the lights worked and his radar gun was calibrated.

We started driving around the city perimeter, making small talk as we went along. I found out Bic's given name was Byron, but an affinity for chewing on pens during toddlerhood saddled him with the nickname of Bic, and it stuck. I also found out his last name, Torbin, was Nordic for "Thor's Bear," which was oddly appropriate given his thunderous presence as well as his sometimes grizzly personality. He told me he wanted to be in law enforcement since he was a child.

"So, Bic, this 'systems thinking' stuff of Rex's … what does the rest of the team think about it?" I tried to sound casual, but Bic saw right through me and belted out a thunderous laugh.

"He told me you'd probably throw the question in at some point, Toby," Bic confessed. He continued, "I'll admit when he first introduced the concept, I was a bit skeptical. Usually, it's the captains or the chief latching onto some management fad brain fart and sending the whole department scurrying down a rabbit hole. So when Rex started talking about using systems thinking and applying it here on the force, I thought maybe he'd been snitching something out of the evidence room, if you know what I mean."

"So you've seen it work, too?" I ventured tentatively. I didn't want to sound like I was undermining Rex's credibility, but I was still struggling with the fact I was being mentored on the finer points of systems thinking and process improvement by a bunch of cops. My logical side wasn't processing this well.

"Seen it work? Hell, I've used it over and over myself!" Bic roared, making me jump as the patrol car swerved. Bic quickly righted the vehicle, mumbling a quick apology for his burst of excitement, and continued. "In law enforcement, we're constantly accused of bein' reactive. Somebody fights; we arrest. Somebody speeds; we ticket 'em. Somebody drinks too much; we take away their license. Rex started challenging our way of thinking about these things a couple of years ago. And his efforts are paying off. Crime in the Metro West is at an all time low."

"I still don't get—" I began.

"Hold that thought," interrupted Bic. He turned on his flashing lights and we were off chasing a sports car which had just whizzed by us through the summer night. The car slowed down and pulled over once the driver noticed we were behind her. Bic programmed the license plate number into the computer mounted to his center console. Other than a couple of prior speeding tickets, there was nothing significant. He turned a knob on the overhead console before he got out of the car, explaining I'd now be able to hear most of the conversation he was having with the motorist. He got out of the car and walked slowly up to the motorist's window. I listened intently to the conversation.

"Good evening. Do you know why I stopped you?" Bic was all business now.

"Was I speeding?" the high-pitched woman's voice came through the speaker.

"Yes, ma'am. I clocked you doing fifty-four in a thirty-five."

"Oh, there's no way I was going that fast. You must be wrong." (Uh-oh, this wasn't starting out well for her.)

"Well, ma'am, that's what the radar said. May I please have your license and registration?"

"You don't really need to do that, do you?" Her voice went up another octave, if possible, and she was speaking more quickly.

"Ma'am, license and registration, please?"

"You just can't write a ticket. My boyfriend said he'd break up with me if I got one more ticket. I don't know what I'll do if I lose him." I heard the sound of sobbing—fake and contrived sobbing—coming through the speaker. This woman was not in line for any acting awards, that much was certain.

"Please ma'am, license and registration. I really don't want to ask you to step out of the car."

"Oh fine," her tone changed from sorrow to anger as I watched her practically throw the paperwork at Bic.

He walked back to the patrol car, shaking his head.

He pulled up the citation screen on his computer and began to type in the information about the speeding ticket.

"Normally, I cut them a break and bring it down to under ten miles per hour … if they cooperate," Bic explained as he continued typing. "If a woman pulls the tears thing on me, I write her up for the full amount. I have no tolerance for drama. Because of her behavior, I'm also writing her up for a seat belt violation, and her left brake light is out."

"Note to self: No tears during traffic stops," I chuckled.

Bic printed out the citations on his printer and pulled out the clipboard to take with him for her to sign. As he explained the process to her, any remorse in the young woman's voice was replaced with outright surliness. Bic stayed professional and even-keeled the entire time, even wishing her a nice evening and safe driving as he left her car. She squealed her tires as she took off. Bic just smiled as he slid into his seat.

"I hope her boyfriend breaks up with her," he mused. "He'll be a better man for it." We both chuckled. We drove off and Bic picked up where he left off.

"About systems thinking, the real trick is to see the relationship between inputs and outputs."

"Funny, we were just having this discussion earlier today," I thought out loud. "I suppose you have an answer for how we see the relationship. My team and I were struggling a little bit with it."

"Do you remember the flash bang devices we used during the training?" I wasn't sure if Bic was changing the subject or building on our current discussion.

"Uh-huh. I don't usually forget something that loud."

"Good. There are a lot of criminals who feel the same way. When we threw the flash bang device into the room, what was the outcome?"

"I suppose it depends on who you ask," I responded. "If you were to ask the role players—the bad guys—they would probably say the outcome was negative. They weren't expecting the bright flash of light or the loud noise. For the SWAT operators, it was positive. They used the distractions to gain control of the situation."

"Grasshopper learns quick," joked Bic. "So any input could create up to two different reactions from the system, right?"

"Yeah, I suppose it's all a matter of perspective, Bic. More flash bangs are good for the system from your point of view. From the criminals' view, not so much."

"That's how we use systems thinking here. We figure out what outcomes we need ... for SWAT, it is a secured building so the investigators can take over. We determine what inputs into the system will help us get the desired output. Inputs will do one of two things to your system: they'll either distract the system from its purpose, or they'll get its attention and move it towards its purpose. Our inputs are knowledge about the stronghold, information about people inside, and our strategy leading us to the safest entry for all involved. When the stronghold system is looked at from our point of view, the flash bang is a system input which gets attention. From the bad guys' point of view, the flash bang is an input into their system which distracts. So what about your job? It sounds like you already know your inputs to get your outputs. But do you know if your inputs distract or get attention?"

Bic waited while I jotted these thoughts down before I lost them.

S.W.A.T. FLYER

Inputs either get attention of the system or they distract the sytem, which impacts the outputs differently.

S.W.A.T. FLYER

Different people in the system will view the inputs differently. This perspective will determine whether inputs get attention or distract.

"We already defined what a successful order looks like and defined all of the inputs by listing them," I looked up from my notebook.

"Great. You identified your inputs," Bic corrected with an emphasis on the word change. "But did you define how they impacted the purchase order? Do you know if those inputs create your desired accomplishment?" At this, I cringed a little while Bic continued. "What are some of the products you sell?"

"We have lines in racquet sports, weight and conditioning, cycling … you name it, seems we try to get into it," I responded.

"OK, what are the most challenging product orders to fill?" Bic continued.

"Probably cycling, because of all of the component parts."

"So if somebody orders more cycling equipment, it'll slow down an order?" He was asking more for clarification, and I nodded. "And a slow order means you don't meet customer demand as fast, right? And distracts your system?"

"Yeah …" I drawled out my response, trying to figure out what was coming next.

"So what other things distract your system from being successful?"

I pondered this for a moment. "If somebody orders more than 20 different items, we have to start a new order form … which takes time. If somebody crosses business units for their order, we have no way to link orders. So if somebody wants both cycling and racquet equipment, we'll have to fill out separate order forms."

"Which again … takes time?" Bic sighed at the mess I was describing.

"Uh-huh," I agreed.

"So anything adding complexity increases your order time and distracts the system," Bic summarized. "Now, here's the question to think about: Is it the inputs themselves—the customer desires—which cause your complexity, or is it the behavior of the inputs once they're in your system—your order processing—that's to blame?"

"Do you mean the inputs can change their behavior once they're in the system?"

"Sure, think about the woman we just stopped. Do you think she behaves like that all the time? I sure hope not. People do weird things when they get stopped for speeding. Everybody in a car is in the environment." Bic waved one arm to indicate the systems environment. "When they choose to break the law and I catch 'em, they enter my system. How they behave when they enter my system determines how I treat 'em, or the output. For example, if a woman turns on the tears, it's an instant ticket in my book … no questions asked."

"So if our customers are ordering things that add complexity to our system, we should quit complaining about the customer order and fix the system … their desires don't and shouldn't change because of our inability to quickly convert their desires into a successful order."

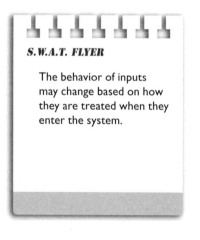

S.W.A.T. FLYER

The behavior of inputs may change based on how they are treated when they enter the system.

"You bet!" Bic cheesed, slapping me on the back. "So, you know your output is a successful customer order. That is your accomplishment. And you know how your inputs influence output. But …"

"But …?" I was a little tentative at this point. We were well past midnight at this point, and the conversation and the ride were beginning to take their toll.

"But … have you figured out how your system messes with the inputs' behavior? In other words, what's happening when you transform the inputs into outputs? You can screw up your systems with a lot of junk if you don't change inputs to outputs as quick as you can."

"Huh?" I was getting confused.

"You know your inputs can change when they're in the system. But how are you changing them? Are you actually adding value to them or are they just sitting in warehouses and on people's desks while your customers get impatient?"

I thought about this comment for a moment. "Since you mentioned it, Bic, we do tend to pass around our customer orders through a lot of hands who do nothing but look at it. Then there are all of the quality checks …"

"Uh oh," Bic began. "I'm smellin' something nasty."

"Wasn't me, buddy. You're the one who had the jumbo burrito at that last break." Bic laughed at my defensiveness.

"Um, yeah, sorry 'bout that, but that's not what I'm talkin' about. Whenever I hear someone mention quality checks, I gotta wonder if it's people just lookin' over someone's shoulder without adding any value. In law enforcement, we do it all the time. A sergeant has to review an officer's report. Then it goes to the Captain. Hell, all they do is rubber-stamp it. Can't tell you the last time one of my men made a big mistake, because I showed 'em how to do it right the first time. Same is true in your business. Show 'em how to do it right the first time and then leave 'em alone. If your transformation step is all about waitin' and checkin' then you ain't gettin' much done. Your customers are pretty smart. In fact, most customers are smarter than you. If you make things uncomfortable, your loyal customers will figure out a workaround. If you are making things too tough, they'll go elsewhere."

I whipped out my notepad and processed what Bic just said before responding.

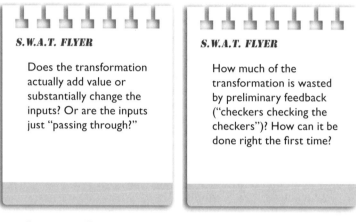

S.W.A.T. FLYER

Does the transformation actually add value or substantially change the inputs? Or are the inputs just "passing through?"

S.W.A.T. FLYER

How much of the transformation is wasted by preliminary feedback ("checkers checking the checkers")? How can it be done right the first time?

"We generally create some new policy every time a customer figures out a new workaround to one of our roadblocks. Our customer guide manual is about three inches thick now," I admitted.

"And does anyone use the manual?" Bic asked with the slightest hint of a smirk.

"Yes ... they make great paperweights and door stops," I laughed.

"Here's a good example of input behavior changing to fit the system." Bic pulled his car to the side of the road on an overpass crossing the city's busiest freeway. Despite the hour, there was still a lot of traffic. "See all of those cars gettin' over into the left-hand lane?"

"Yeah, I do ... but why? There doesn't appear to be any construction up ahead ... at least I don't see any signs."

"That's because all the signs were taken down yesterday," Bic noted wryly. "But for the past four months, the two right-hand lanes've been closed 'bout a half-mile up. The inputs—the drivers in their cars—have been conditioned to get as far left as possible. It'll probably take another week before the drivers figure out the road is open now. They'll adjust their driving back to the way it was before. But for now, the inputs've been conditioned to drive a certain way on this road."

"That's why Evan is always so grumpy," I mused, halfway to myself.

"Who's Evan?" Bic asked.

"He's on my team, and he leads the customer complaint group," I answered. "Because we have no good online order system, a lot of our repeat customers use him to place orders because they've learned from sending him complaints … well … he just handles things. So they bypass the Call Center and just e-mail him directly with orders. It drives our executive crazy because it flies in the face of her demands. She wants the orders sent back through the normal channels." I jotted down my observation before putting my notebook away.

S.W.A.T. FLYER

Inputs will change their own behaviors based on how they've been treated in the system in the past.

For the rest of the night, we went from call to call. There was a drunk driver, a hit-and-run, an apartment fire, a rescue call assist, a potential fight at a local restaurant, and a couple more traffic stops. For each of these, Bic demonstrated how the outputs of the people involved were influenced by their inputs.

By 7:30 Saturday morning, I was snoring loudly in my own

bed, just as my wife was waking up.

"How was the ride along?" she asked.

"SNORT… sputter… mmmmm-hmmmm… SNORE," was my answer. But even asleep, my brain was racing with all kinds of information I hoped I could retain until Monday.

Chapter 8

> *"If the first button of one's coat is wrongly buttoned, all the rest will be crooked."*
>
> -Giordano Bruno

"So we need to figure out the behavior of these inputs and isolate the behaviors we want to change?" Elena repeated a summary of my lengthy explanation at our next meeting. My ride-along with Bic from the previous weekend had left me with plenty of ammunition to prepare for this meeting.

"This actually makes sense," Evan added. "When I think about where the system breaks down, my team feels the heat of the feedback loop since our customers tell us when things are going wrong."

"OK, so what next?" Seth asked.

"Well, we're going to do some good old-fashioned data gathering which would make your Six Sigma buddies proud." I actually made Seth grin. "And we're going to start with brainstorming to figure out where our system breaks down. We know the desired outcome is a successful order, but what are the things that keep us from getting there?"

The team wasted no time in throwing out ideas. A lot of them were issues we'd already discussed; nevertheless, it was important we capture them to make our order-taking system better. After we finished brainstorming, we talked about each issue. We figured out early on that systems behavior had to be observable to be fixed. Every once in a while, Seth or Rachel tried to throw in their gut intuitions, and we challenged them on it. If we couldn't see what was going on, or if the feedback loop didn't sniff it out, we knew we'd have a hard time justifying it to management. In the end, we figured out there were only about a dozen notable problems preventing the Call Center from completing a successful order. Given this, we defined a successful order as one that:

- ❏ Was completed in one call

- ❏ Was completed in a timely fashion (on average 30 seconds per item ordered plus two minutes per call)

- ❏ Had all inventory in stock

- ❏ Would not be slowed down by customer issues (bad credit or incomplete data)

- ❏ The customer felt satisfied their needs had been met.

These five criteria became the basis for our feedback loop. If anything about the call was unsuccessful, these would be the alarm which isolated the problem. We also figured out that in order to see what made a system work, we had to figure out what could break a system. Most of the time, we noted, the things stressing the system the most were variants from the five criteria. Sometimes there were overloads to the criteria, though. For example, if we were receiving too many orders at once, while they might all be good orders, that could stress the system. We were lucky because Evan told us the data had been tracked and stored for months on "bad orders," but nobody ever knew what to do about this information.

We looked at the data already collected and made some
surprising discoveries. First of all, we found out the Call Center
was very inconsistent with lengths of call times, but they
appeared to fall into two categories: really, really short calls and
really, really long calls. It also seemed the company standards
we had identified were being ignored. Part of the reason for this
was each team in the Call Center was rewarding something
different. Some teams rewarded shortened call times more, so the
customer service representatives were getting just the most basic
information and getting off the call. Of course, this generally
meant they had to call back later to clarify, but nobody was
tracking rewards or penalties for follow-up calls. Other teams
were being rewarded on customer feedback and were being
encouraged to take an inordinately long time on the calls to make
the customer feel good. Their performance stats were terrible, but
the customer feedback was very positive.

Second, we found out customer credit problems were one
of the least frequent issues. Then Evan suggested we factor in
the cost of each issue. When we did, the impact of customer
credit soared past all of the other problems identified. Evidently,
customer credit issues were popping up on the largest orders from

the dealers because Finance was checking consumer data rather than commercial data, so the CSR thought the customer had good credit when in reality, the CSR didn't have the right kind of information available.

The last problem we found was with the inventory system. I was under the assumption the Call Center had "real time" data available to them; in other words, what was actually in inventory was reflected on the information screens. I found out the warehouse updated information in the database only once a week (twice if month end-fell during the week), so the information could be days old … and very stale.

The team was quickly getting dejected over these discoveries.

"It's no use," Rachel complained. "Almost all of our key problems are outside of our control. How can we be successful when Finance and Inventory won't give us the information we need when we need it?"

"As you pointed out, Toby," Evan jumped in, "these problems just motivate our customers to find ways of working around them … provided they don't leave and go to another distributor altogether."

"Yeah, our inputs are all screwed up," Seth moaned. "There's no way we can transform them into the output we want. So the inputs are finding their own ways of getting what they want … whether it fits into our model or not."

"The problem is, we're running out of time," Elena stressed. Everybody's facial expressions were grim. At that moment my cell phone rang and made everybody jump. I apologized as I put a dollar into the "No cell phone during meetings" penalty jar and excused myself into the hallway. Normally, I would've just let it go to voice-mail, but I noticed it was from Rex. My intuition told me I should take it.

"Did I catch you at a bad time?" Rex asked quickly but didn't wait for me to answer. "Look, I don't know if you can make it, but the SWAT team was given a great opportunity for a full practice tonight at the abandoned mall. We're going to run a sniper/hostage scenario with negotiators."

"You just now found out about it?" I was skeptical. "These things take weeks to plan out."

"Oh we've been planning it, but it kept getting caught in red tape from the city's planning and zoning commission. You know how we government bureaucrats work. Anyway, we've had the guys on alert and just got the green light today. The Captain says you can watch again if you want. I'll even let you listen in on the negotiators."

"Oooookaaaay," I drawled. "When and where?"

"Meet me here at the police station at sixteen hundred hours if you can get off work early enough. Call and confirm at fifteen hundred hours."

"Roger. Copy. Over. Adios." I responded.

"Something important?" Rachel quizzed when I returned. "You're always the cell phone cop around here."

"Let's just say my intuition told me the phone call might hold the answer to our problem," I said mysteriously.

"And did it?" Evan inquired.

"I'll let you know tomorrow." My response left them with puzzled looks on their faces.

Near the center of the metropolitan area stood an abandoned mall. Since the city's expansion outward to the suburbs, new malls had sprung up on the southwest and northeastern suburbs, leaving business at the City Centre Shopping Mall a mere trickle. When the anchor stores either pulled out or went bankrupt, the smaller shops followed suit, and the mall officially closed a few months ago. Now I had to chuckle at the dilapidated mall sign touting the state's largest Gap … a consumer's double entendre if ever there was one.

Rex and I pulled into the mall parking lot around 5:00. It was obvious the teams had mobilized quickly for this training, but even given the short notice, everybody seemed well organized. The operators were already in their gear, and the command staff swiftly briefed their teams on the upcoming scenario. A shooter had opened fire in the mall, killing three people and wounding dozens of others before barricading himself in the Shooters Haven Video Arcade—again, what is it with the double meanings? The scenario began with the negotiators establishing telephone contact with the shooter, determining his location, and keeping him distracted while the SWAT operators cover the EMT crew attempting to recover the wounded.

The negotiators were stationed in a separate trailer out in the mall parking lot. Rex suggested I hang out in the negotiators' trailer since a lot of the real action would occur there. (Again, I had a feeling there was a reason behind this, but Rex was going to make me discover it on my own.) A local psychologist was playing the role of the mall shooter, as he was able to build a strong sense of realism into the motives of such a criminal. I listened as the three negotiators worked together to gather information from the shooter and about the shooter. The commanders had set up role players as simulated family members of the shooter, each one able to provide pivotal pieces of information to the negotiators … if the right questions were asked. The negotiators needed to work together to figure out the motive behind the shooter's actions and determine what drove him to this point. It was fascinating to watch them work together. They seemed to read each other's minds, and the way the information flowed among them made them appear almost telepathic. On two of the walls, there were large marker boards, and the negotiator on the phone with the shooter would write information she gathered from him. The other two wrote pieces of information they found from the internet (yeah, the police even set up "fake data" on the internet) and phone calls with his "family and acquaintances."

Eventually, despite their best efforts, the negotiations broke down and the SWAT operators were called in to take out the sniper. Finally, I had the opportunity to talk to one of the negotiators who appeared to be taking a rest.

"That was interesting," I offered in the way of a conversation starter.

"To put it mildly," she responded, the weariness evident in her voice after a couple of hours of intense conversation. I introduced myself as Rex's cousin.

"I'm Detective Alycia Winslow, but you can call me Aly," she extended her hand. "Rex told me about you. Said he's been trying to help you figure out how to use systems thinking. You work for SysteMuscle here in town, right?"

"Yeah," I answered halfheartedly. "It's not been going as smoothly or easily as you're all able to apply it here on the SWAT team, though." I hit an unintended nerve.

"Easy?" she flared. "This job is far from easy, as I hope you just saw."

"I'm sorry," I apologized. "I didn't mean to imply it wasn't difficult. It's kind of like figure skating, though. You all make it look easy when you communicate so well together. You know what you're pursuing and you go after it. When the SWAT operators yell, 'Dominate!' I know they mean it and they've earned it. My team, on the other hand, seems to trip over their own shoe laces."

"Give me an example," Aly coaxed, relaxing into our conversation.

"Well, today we were figuring out how our inputs enter the system. We know what we want for an output: a successful customer order. We even know how to convert inputs to outputs. As we started talking about all of the potential distractions to our system, we figured out most of them are out of our control." I went on to explain the issues with inventory and credit we had uncovered earlier in the day.

"Your systems are missing SWAT," Aly diagnosed, rather matter-of-factly.

"No, I've been applying the systems thinking lessons I've been learning from your teams," I countered, ever-so-slightly defensive.

"I'm sure you have," she replied, "but I'm talking about something beyond the systems thinking concepts Rex has been sharing with you. This is SWAT—Systems Working All Together. It's systems thinking on steroids. It's getting each individual system to start working with the others. What you've been learning from Rex has been great, and you certainly need to learn and apply how one single system works. But it's not enough to stop at your own system. Your inputs are somebody else's outputs. Your outputs become inputs for another system elsewhere. You absolutely have to start looking at your system as part of the larger environment—why it's critical to get your Systems Working All Together. Your Call Center system is reliant on the system that's going on in the customer's brain. It is also dependent on your inventory system and your credit system. Every system has interdependencies with other systems in its environment. Here on the SWAT team, we are constantly reminded of ways our systems work together."

"How so?" Aly had piqued my curiosity.

"For starters, just within the negotiation team, you noticed we had three systems working simultaneously. We had one negotiator working with the perpetrator—the person who is holed up somewhere and we're trying to talk him or her into a peaceful resolution. We have another negotiator who is trying to gain intelligence on this individual from other sources—family and friends and the internet. A third negotiator may be working with the SWAT commander or synthesizing input from all the other sources. In other words they make sure our systems are working all together."

"OK, but isn't this really just one system with multiple roles?" I challenged.

"You could look at it that way," Aly conceded. "But when you look at the bigger picture, you see where all of the pieces start to fit together. The dispatcher has their set of processes to convert a 911 call input into the output of a mission for the command team. The command team then has to take the information from the dispatchers—their input—and convert it into an output strategy for the negotiators, the entry teams, and the investigative detectives. All of these teams have to work together or none of their outputs will hold up in court when the prosecutors are trying to convict criminals."

Aly went over to the white board and drew a picture to show all of the parts:

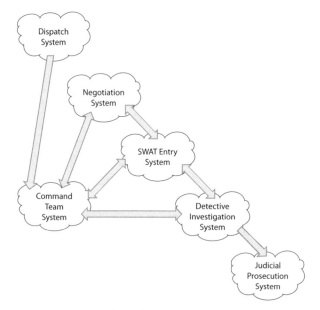

And there it was, right in front of me. If we were going to make this process improvement project successful, we were going to have to apply SWAT beyond just the Call Center. We would have to approach the managers of the customer credit and finance department as well as the inventory control department. While we were at it, we needed to figure out where our output—the successful customer order—became an input to other areas in the company. This was the missing accomplishment.

"You OK, Toby? You look a little bleary-eyed," Aly pushed up a chair behind me, and I sat down.

"I think I'm just overwhelmed. How do you make all of these pieces fit together? I mean, it sounds like SWAT is good in theory, and I can't argue with what you've just shown me. I'm just trying to figure out how I'm going to make it happen. A lot of the systems you just drew are outside of your control."

"Fair enough. Our teams had to go through a lot of communication to get this all figured out, and we're lucky Rex saw the big picture and drew this model for us. When we get the order to answer a call needing the SWAT team, each team knows how their words and actions can affect the next team down the line."

"How did you get to the point where you made your systems work all together? Certainly it wasn't as simple as Rex drawing a picture and all of you saluting?"

At this Aly laughed. "Oh no, we went through our share of screw-ups along the way. We started by talking to the prosecutors and finding out about cases they'd lost where a SWAT entry team was involved, both our team and other teams. Rex took a few SWAT operators to interview county and state prosecutors whenever there was down time in the department. Keep in mind, he did all of this while he was just an operator himself, but the chief took note of his initiative. From there, we compiled some of the main reasons why cases were lost when they should've been won."

"So, in other words, he backed into what the investigators and detectives were providing to the prosecutors," I said, pointing at the final arrow between systems.

"Uh-huh," Aly agreed. "Then we talked to the detectives and investigators. They told us what they needed from the commanders, the entry teams, and the negotiators to provide the prosecutors with the best evidence possible to win the case."

"Then it just becomes a case of moving backward through the system until you've accounted for every input-output relationship between systems, right?" I was beginning to understand the scope of what we were going to need to accomplish. Aly nodded her agreement to my clarification.

"In order to achieve Systems Working All Together, those same systems will need to communicate with each other," Aly added.

I sighed. "And therein lies the rub." Somehow, quoting Shakespeare can make any problem seem more manageable. Now if I could just find a quote to make the solution workable.

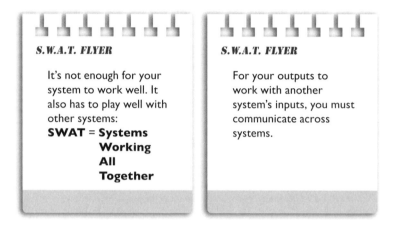

S.W.A.T. FLYER

It's not enough for your system to work well. It also has to play well with other systems:

SWAT = Systems
Working
All
Together

S.W.A.T. FLYER

For your outputs to work with another system's inputs, you must communicate across systems.

Chapter 9

"All that is necessary for the triumph of evil is that good men do nothing."

-Edmund Burke

"I was afraid you were going to say that," Evan sighed, when he heard and saw my explanation about SWAT. All but Elena were a little surprised when I revealed my source for the coaching, but the overall reaction was more of appreciation than apprehension.

"But Toby's right," Elena defended. "We've already proven to ourselves we must have the other managers on board."

"That's not the question," Rachel shot back. "What's going to motivate these people to listen to us? They all have departments and teams and problems and budgets and projects. We're just going to waltz in and say, 'Excuse me, can we create more work for you to make our lives easier?'"

"We don't have a choice," Seth jumped in. "And we do have a bargaining chip with these managers, Rachel."

"And what would that be?"

"When you look at our SWAT diagram, we're not just dependent on them for good data. Eventually, they're dependent on us. For example, we can guarantee Finance will get better information from us if we have a successful order. Rona won't let us bill the client until the order can successfully go out the door, and you should hear the supervisors from Finance complain about the size of their accounts receivable. There are so many outstanding payments for goods; if we could collect more quickly on all of our orders, it'd improve our cash flow by 40 percent each of the first three months."

"Can you prove it?" I asked, incredulous Seth was able to produce such a specific figure.

"I can," Elena stood up. "Seth shared this with me after our meeting yesterday, and while you were spending time with the SWAT team last night, we started doing some research on this information. I think Finance would jump at the chance to improve their cash flow."

"I don't understand why Rona created these policies. I found out she's also done the same thing with our issues with Inventory," Evan offered in an unamused tone. "It's almost like she's trying to sabotage the entire company."

"Or maybe just me," I muttered under my breath, audible to nobody but myself. I knew from the beginning Rona wanted to get rid of me; she had made her intentions abundantly clear. I was wondering if I were out of the equation, whether the team could actually be successful. Maybe this project was Rona's sacrificial lamb to get me out of the way.

"Can we write Rona out of the processes?" asked Elena, only halfway jokingly, as if reading my mind.

"I wish," I admitted. Rona couldn't just be out to sabotage me, as much as my paranoid mind had been conditioned to think so. She must honestly think she's doing good somehow. "Maybe Rona believes by adding these steps to the processes, she's helping."

"Helping?" Evan countered. "You've got to be kidding."

"Sometimes people manage by exception. They try to corral all of the variables to the system they don't like, and instead of streamlining all of the processes which already work relatively well, they spend their energy attempting to manage only the ones not working well. Eventually what does work well breaks because it's been ignored too long," I offered in the way of explanation, which certainly sounded better than suggesting Rona was out to get me personally.

We spent the rest of our time together developing a game plan for meeting with the managers of Finance and Inventory. There was considerable debate over our approach with these managers. Our first thought was to present to both managers together since the problems were parallel between the departments; however, Evan challenged us to look at it from the managers' point of view. Neither would want to sit through the other one's issues; we would be lucky to find a time to schedule them together in one room in order to get them on board before our looming September 1st deadline.

The second argument arose on the order and content of the presentations. Rachel wanted to start at the beginning with everything and "take them on a journey" with us. Since Seth and Elena had researched the quantitative impacts to both departments, we decided to take the "executive approach" and share the bottom line impact up front. Then we would peel back the details so they could see how we arrived at our solutions and conclusions. Because our presentations to both managers would occur just days before our big presentation, we needed to make sure we had solid commitment from both managers to make the changes we wanted. Therefore, our last order of business with each manager would have to be to "ask for the sale" and make firm commitments on dates and resources, with the caveat the September 1st meeting would be the deciding point for whether or not we could proceed.

We proceeded to set up the meetings. As with my efforts with Howard from Facilities a few weeks ago, we worked through the administrative assistants to get time on their already busy schedules. When we explained what we were doing, both admins seemed pleased to help, as it appeared they were the unlucky recipients of the extra work caused by the broken systems.

Both meetings went exceptionally well. Each of the managers had intuitively known there was a breakdown in how the Call Center interacted with their departments, but neither could put their finger on the problem to pinpoint it. We were very careful not to be confrontational in the meeting as we didn't want either manager to feel they were walking into an "us vs. them" ambush. When we explained how our solutions could improve the performance measures for their departments, we had both managers promising resources and throwing budget dollars our way. Their excitement was encouraging, and we would need it to finalize our executive presentation. Each manager committed people from his or her department to help us define our solutions to ensure we had Systems Working All Together. Elena and Evan took the lead on the Finance and Accounting interfaces, while Seth and Rachel handled the Inventory dependencies. I made sure all four of them continued to communicate with each other.

For the final presentation, we began by defining the desired accomplishments (outputs) for the Call Center. Then we shared how we would measure the success of the outputs (feedback loop). From there we moved into the needed inputs and how we would have to transform those inputs into the outputs we wanted. Finally, we moved into the environment and showed all of the other systems within the company which had major impacts with the Call Center. We focused primarily on places where we overlapped with Finance and Inventory Control, since those had the largest impacts and they were also the areas where we had already talked to the other managers.

The day before the presentation, I could tell the events of the past several weeks were beginning to converge, but I couldn't pinpoint why I was feeling that way. While my team members were feeling more relaxed and prepared and engaged, I was getting more tense and anxious. I didn't need to wait long to find out why.

"Toby, I'd like a word with you," Rona was using her syrupy voice, which meant that 1) I was in trouble; and 2) I'd feel like

I needed a shower later. We stepped into her office and she motioned for me to close the door.

"I'm very disappointed in you. I've had complaints from both the managers of Finance and Inventory about you and your team. It seems you've been bothering them," Rona began her matronly tirade, sounding more like a scolding grandmother than an executive. However, I was used to it. This was, after all, part of her passive-aggressive technique. Rona almost never raised her voice. She used condescension and innuendo to try to make a person feel about three inches tall. Today her tool of choice was character sabotage.

"Um, Rona?" I finally interrupted in the middle of her droning about my impending failure. I decided to mirror the same condescending tone she had. After all, I really had nothing to lose in her apparent efforts to bring me down. "I talked to both managers earlier today. I find it very strange neither one has said a thing to me or my team about being annoyed. Could it be you just misunderstood them? As you say, we all make mistakes."

Bull's-eye. Rona stopped dead in her tracks and turned a couple of shades of red before regaining her composure and speaking again.

"Perhaps you didn't understand the coaching I was trying to give you. You will greatly upset these managers if you pull them into your presentation tomorrow, not to mention what you'll be doing to the entire organization by adding onto the scope of what I thought was a very easy-to-understand assignment. I guess people with simple minds just can't do simple tasks."

Then her real motivation hit me.

"You're scared, aren't you?" I countered. "You know if Doug likes our presentation tomorrow, he'll start rethinking all of the crap you've been feeding him about me for the past several months, as well as all of the so-called 'improvements' you've implemented. It's not my credibility on the line; it's yours."

She faltered over the accusation while she thought up a response, but I could tell I had hit the one nerve she didn't want me to hit. I wasn't about to wait for her to regroup, and I wasn't caring about consequence anymore. What I wanted was to regain my self-esteem, and it was now or never to speak up. "My team has plowed through a ton of difficult challenges in the past couple of months. We've worked harder than any team in the history of SysteMuscle, at least any team since I've been here, which—if I may remind you—is longer than you have."

She again started to speak, but I cut her off.

"You saddled me with the four most difficult people you knew from the Call Center. Why you did it I can only guess. Did you want to protect the processes you created, or did you just want to see me fail so badly you set me up for failure at the company's expense?"

I took a deep breath, not lingering long enough for her to answer before I continued to unleash.

"What you didn't anticipate was deep down they want to do their jobs well. You didn't think I had the skill or talent to tap into their passion. So after we started showing results, you started having doubts about whether you'd look good in the end."

Again, the shades of red returned to her face, brighter than ever, but I still wasn't going to let her get a word in edgewise.

"Rona, I want to see this team succeed, and if the only way they can succeed is without me, then so be it. I'm not going to let you sabotage their efforts. We've done something very good for SysteMuscle, and we put our own egos aside to do it, something you could never understand. We've all worked too damn hard for you to throw up road blocks because you feel threatened. Then, if we do succeed, you'd probably waltz in to steal the credit and gloat. Well, not today and not on my watch."

I walked over to the door, opened it, and then turned around.

"But let me tell you one more thing: you may wear the title of an executive, but you will never be half the leader these four people are."

SLAM!

I walked over to my desk. Most of the people in my area were away from their desks, so I grabbed a box and took a few personal effects with me on my way out the door. I told our department receptionist I was just de-cluttering, and I was taking the rest of the afternoon off. If any of the team needed me, I could be reached on my cell, which coincidentally rang the second I mentioned it.

"You ready for the big presentation tomorrow?" Rex's chipper voice was just about more than I could handle.

"I suppose," I answered tiredly while walking to my car. Telling off Rona had expended a burst of energy reserves I didn't know existed.

"What's wrong?" Rex cut in. "You don't sound like yourself."

"I think I just quit my job."

"You WHAT?!" Rex's voice thundered in my ear as I loaded the box in the trunk and closed the door.

"You heard me," I deadpanned. "And, if you don't mind, I'm not in the mood to talk about it." I clicked the END button on my cell phone before Rex had a chance to respond. I had progressed about three miles out of the SysteMuscle corporate headquarters when I saw flashing lights in my rear-view mirror. It was Rex.

"Wow, and I'm always complaining there's never a cop around when I want one," I quipped, trying to sound more chipper than I felt.

"Follow me," Rex commanded as he approached my window, appearing somewhat more than irritated with me. "And so help me, God, if you deviate one inch from behind my car, I'm arresting you for chronic stupidity. Now drive." He stalked back to his car and pulled out in front of me. Dutifully, I turned the ignition and followed him to our favorite watering hole. Rex was often out and about in the community, so nobody would think twice about his car being parked at a bar in the middle of the day. His integrity and reputation were well known throughout town, and most people who mattered knew we often came here to talk.

"OK, talk," Rex barked after ordering a pair of Diet Cokes.

"I'll tell you when to shut up."

I started by telling Rex about my conversation with Aly and finally understanding the essence of SWAT. I shared with him my team's preparations over the past week, of getting the Finance and Inventory teams supportive and on board. I wound up with my unfortunate conversation with Rona from an hour prior.

"I had to do it, Rex," I wrapped up. "If I didn't, there was no way the team was going to be allowed to be successful tomorrow. I told you the only reason she put me on this assignment was to undermine my credibility with Doug. You yourself questioned the assignment when I first told you about it. She just didn't think I'd be successful at pulling it off. When her attempt at sabotaging me failed today, it was just as though something inside clicked. I can't and won't continue to let her emasculate me."

"I suppose you're right," Rex agreed, and then playfully added, "that's what we have wives for, right?"

"I screwed up, didn't I?"

"You tell me."

"Well, there goes Molly's doctoral program. She'll probably need to go back to work while I'm looking for another job. She really wanted this, and now I've messed it up for her." A sense of overwhelming dread filled me as I thought about sharing this news with my wife.

"Can you fix it?"

"What? You mean go back and grovel to Rona? I doubt it." I explained the conversation in a little more detail, including the door slam, which made him flinch.

"You can't let your team down. I know you think you're doing the right thing by skipping out of the presentation tomorrow, but you are an integral part of their system. If change is the output, and if success is the feedback loop, then you, my friend, are a key input. There will be a huge gaping hole in the room tomorrow if their leader isn't in there with them."

"I just don't know," I shook my head. "Rona could've gone to HR already and terminated me."

126

"Do you think she did?"

"Probably not. She'll want to have the satisfaction of announcing it tomorrow in the meeting when I don't show up."

"Then it's all the more important you show up with your head held high," Rex impressed upon me. "Just pretend like the whole thing—"

Rex's cell rang, and as he took the call, his facial expression grew grim.

"That was Bic. We're serving a search warrant on a suspected meth lab tonight. Just got the orders. We've been anticipating it for weeks, but the intel just came in. We can get the entire ring and their boss if we strike at sunset tonight." Rex stood up and started to leave, but turned around to face me. "Promise me you'll be at that meeting tomorrow, Toby. I can't explain it, but I need to hear you promise before I can walk out of here."

I like being known as a man of my word, and lying has never been a skill I've ever aspired to master. As I muttered the words, "I promise" they just seemed to fall to the floor. The look of disappointment on Rex's face showed me he knew they were hollow words. This time, he was the one who shrugged as he turned and sprinted to his car. After paying for our Diet Cokes and heading out to my car, I left a message with Molly to tell her I wouldn't be home until late. She knew I had the big presentation tomorrow, so she would assume I'd be at the office. I let her assume that. As long as I was being dishonest at the moment, I figured I was on a streak.

There was a park right on the outskirts of our sprawling suburb. Since the rest of the town grew in the opposite direction, this park had become virtually ignored. Some of the corporate neighbors had converted part of it to a prairie grass restoration reserve. There were numerous winding trails through the park, which allowed me to do the two things I liked doing most: walking and thinking. I shut off my cell phone (something I almost never do) and meandered through the trails. I was disappointed in myself for having flown off the handle at Rona, especially right before the team's big presentation. I was disappointed in myself for letting down my wife. I was disappointed in myself for letting down my team and my company.

The sun was setting, and the brilliant colors cast a stark contrast against the dull gray I was feeling inside. After walking around the trails for the better part of an hour, I sat and thought about what Rex had said. The entire time I had worked on this project, I'd managed to distance myself from the team emotionally. Even when we were getting along, I had kept them at arm's length. Was Rex right? Was I really an integral part of the system? I hadn't felt that way for a long time. I used to love working at SysteMuscle, but since the day Rona arrived, it seemed like I had shut down. I was no longer an input into the system. I'd stayed there because my wife had needed me to, because I felt I had to, not because I'd wanted to.

But I had to admit, the past few weeks it felt like I'd been adding value again. Yeah, there were times where it had been tough to drag myself out of bed and head into work, but since the start of the project, I really began to see some of the old spark. I thought about my new friends on the SWAT team and the lessons they'd shared with me. While I'm sure Rex had encouraged it to a degree, they all provided me with valuable pieces to the puzzle, just as I had needed them. I learned to look at my job in a new light, and there was so much I could do to help SysteMuscle become a vital player in the industry once again.

But then there was Rona. Doug had hired her so he could spend more time avoiding the duties of being an executive, but maybe his internal compass had been messed up as much as mine. Doug is an entrepreneur, not a manager. Heck, I'd been telling him as much since I'd been hired. Maybe he felt compelled to bring her on board because of my feedback. My input into the organizational structure resulted in a very disastrous output. I'm not sure why Rona appeared to be threatened by me, but she certainly used her insecurities to undermine my business relationship with Doug as well as taking sadistic pleasure in making my life miserable.

Thinking of Rona made me acutely aware of the chill in the air since the sun had now set. I'd been wandering the park trails for hours. I went back to my car to grab a jacket and saw my cell phone lying on the dashboard. Remembering I'd turned it off so I could be alone with my thoughts, I figured it was time to reconnect again with the world at large ... both here and now in the park, and in the other areas of my life. If Rona wanted a fight tomorrow, I was going to give her one. I owed it to Rex to fight. I owed it to my wife to fight. I owed it to my team to fight. But most importantly, I owed it to myself to fight. I'd learned a thing or two about playing office politics guerilla style. While Rona was bossy, domineering, and passive-aggressive, she was also not very smart at human relations. The way she had managed me during this whole project, especially today, proved she didn't have a lot of mental or social bandwidth to fall back on; she relied on her old tricks to get her way. Well it was about time somebody turned the tables on her. If I got fired in the process, so be it. I had kept enough documentation on her behavior to make her life miserable on the way out.

"Bring it on, Rona," I muttered as I turned my cell phone back on. The old Toby was back, and he had a fire in his belly.

My phone's voice mail alert went off almost immediately. I had missed fifteen calls, all of them coming in the last half hour. Something was wrong. Since most of them were from my wife, Molly, I called her first.

"Hello?" she answered her phone. I could tell she had been crying, and my first thought was someone had told her about my discussion with Rona. I could handle a problem like that. What I couldn't handle was what she said next.

"Where have you been, Toby? I have half the town looking for you. Rex has been shot."

Chapter 10

"He who chooses the beginning of the road chooses the place it leads to. It is the means that determine the ends."

-Harry Emerson Fosdick

I'm not exactly sure how I arrived at the hospital. From the second Molly told me the news, everything seemed to melt into a surreal mix of soggy slow-motion and fuzzy fast-forward. It's said in times of extreme trauma or stress, people have been known to have almost out-of-body experiences where they're able to observe themselves acting and speaking like some kind of performance. I was on some sort of existential auto-pilot.

I vaguely remember the stinging sensation in my eyes while I was driving to the hospital, very grateful not to meet any of the guys on the force, given the number of traffic laws I broke on my way. To this day, though, I wouldn't be able to tell you the route I took to arrive. Rex was more than just my cousin; he was my best friend. I couldn't imagine getting through a week without numerous phone calls and getting together at least once for a chat.

Making it to the hospital, I screeched my car to a stop in the first open spot I could find, not really paying much attention to the location. The nurse at the Intensive Care Surgical Unit check-in was a vague blur, but she saw my name on the approved list of visitors and had an orderly escort me to Rex's room.

My brain actively reengaged as I suddenly found myself by Rex's bedside, but it was empty; Rex wasn't there. His wife, Wendy, was in the room. Everything you hear about the silent worries of the spouse of a law enforcement officer was written on her face, and there were a few more lines on it than the last time I saw her. The tightrope she'd been walking between dread and expectation didn't prevent her from smiling, standing up, and hugging me. I told myself I was going to be strong for her sake, but it didn't prevent the tears from starting to flow.

"Wendy, I came as soon as Molly told me." I must have glanced over at the empty bed a little too apprehensively, for Wendy perceived my reluctance to ask the obvious question. She is every bit as perceptive as her husband.

"He's still in surgery," her simple explanation coincided with my audible sigh of relief. She handed me a tissue. "Wh… What happened?" She began recounting the story about the drug bust.

"With all of the protective padding he wears, the bullet managed to find about the only spot of unprotected flesh where it could enter and do some serious harm. It tore through his arm and entered his chest from the side, lodging next to his lung. We're lucky, though. A couple more inches and it would have hit his heart."

Finally, my logical side caught up with my emotions. "But how? How did it happen? I've been hanging around Rex and his team long enough to know none of them ever does anything without backup. The stack is everything to him."

"It happened while they were doing the secondary sweep, when they thought everything was clear. During their entry, there was just enough of a warning the head of the drug ring climbed into the rafters and hid in an old covered feedbox in the barn loft. They thought they had everybody centralized and in custody. During the shouts of 'clear' and 'dominate,' Rex thought he saw something in the rafters. The 'something' must have realized he'd been spotted because he shot without warning while Rex was scanning the rafters. Tadd figured out what happened immediately and fired about a dozen rounds into the loft while the other guys took care of Rex. The gang leader is very, very dead." She emphasized the last sentence with a combination of triumph and indignation that anybody would think to harm her husband.

"Is Rex … is he going to be OK?"

"The doctor came in before you arrived. He said there was still about a half hour of surgery left and then some recovery time in the operating room before they moved him back here. It was touch-and-go for a while, but Rex is tough… all of you Donovan boys are."

"I wasn't feeling very tough tonight," I admitted tearfully. "Given how I left things with Rex earlier, I don't know what I would have done if he … if …." I couldn't finish the sentence.

"Well, there was no 'if.' Rex never even lost consciousness until they put him under here at the hospital for surgery. The guys had to fight to keep him still. As a matter of fact, he dictated two short notes to the medic. Mine was a bunch of gushy husband-and-wife stuff. Do you want to read yours?"

"A note? Rex left me a note?"

"And … like most Donovan boys … you're a little slow at listening to what's being said. Yes, a note." Wendy handed me the piece of paper folded multiple times with my name on the outside fold. I held it in my hands, almost worried to unfold it, fearing the worst scolding my cousin—my hero—could give me, a scolding which I knew I deserved. Wendy looked at me expectantly, so I slowly unfolded it and read the few short sentences aloud.

> Toby
> Thanks for coming to be with Wendy at the hospital. Sorry to be a bother the night before your big presentation. I know you'll knock 'em dead. One last piece of advice: Watch out for unwanted inputs into your system. Bullets Suck.
> Rex

Wendy and I both shared an unexpected but much needed laugh at the wisdom of the sage.

A short while later, numerous nurses came into the room and began prepping the equipment which would track Rex's vital signs. The doctor also came in and said Rex made it through surgery. He was going to let Rex recover here in the ICU rather than in the operating recovery room, as originally planned. Wendy hugged the doctor and thanked him warmly.

After a couple minutes more, Rex was wheeled into the room. He was unconscious, but he didn't look too terrible for a man who'd been seriously shot and had undergone major invasive surgery. The doctor explained the blood loss had been minimal because of the immediate medical attention he had received at the site and the quick response from the ambulance crew. He had tubes and wires everywhere, but I could tell from all of the machines and monitors his body was doing what it was supposed to do.

I excused myself to phone Molly with an update. While it was now well after midnight, my wife had insisted I call her as soon as I knew something. She asked if I was coming home, knowing about my presentation in the morning. I suggested she go back to sleep, and I would try to catch some shut-eye here at the hospital. I knew I couldn't go anywhere until Rex regained consciousness, and it didn't matter that the future of my job hung in the balance.

After I returned to the room, Wendy was busy around Rex's bed, attempting to make him as comfortable as she could. She looked exhausted.

"I'm surprised Rex's team isn't in a stack outside his door," I mused.

"That was Rex's idea. He was a little upset nobody was able to reach you before he went into surgery, but he knew the best thing for me would be as few people as possible hanging around. His men are wonderful and they would follow him into any battle, but in their dedication to their team leader, they can forget some things that matter to family members. I mean, can you imagine

Bic here at his bedside? The nurses would have to sedate him. He'd be wound up tighter than a top. He'd be so concerned for Rex he would be in the way and probably wear me out. We also have a lot of friends who are wonderful at social gatherings, but a critical hospital visit wouldn't be something they'd have the stomach for."

I hugged her again and then encouraged her to go make any calls she needed to make to family and to Rex's team. I stayed at the foot of his bed, just watching all of the monitors. The readouts assured me everything in Rex's internal systems was going to be fine. Even unconscious in a hospital bed, Rex was a living case study of the power of SWAT.

Wendy and I talked throughout the night. She asked about Molly's doctoral program and schooling. I asked how their kids were doing. We talked about jobs and home projects. About five in the morning, I convinced her (with the help of a nurse) to get some rest. I promised her I'd stay for a couple more hours before I'd have to head to work. I knew I had a fresh change of clothing and a toiletry kit at the office gym, so by the time my team saw me, it wouldn't look like I'd been up all night.

About an hour later, I found myself getting restless and wanting to walk around. I stretched my legs around the room and eventually found myself staring out the window. The same sun whose disappearance I'd watched twelve hours prior was now preparing for reentrance. Even the sun and earth understood the relationships of systems thinking, I thought as I appreciated the view from Rex's window. The fatigue I'd experienced over the past day was catching up to me, but I was still acutely alert.

Alert, yes. Ready, no. Suddenly I felt a pointy object lightly strike the back of my neck. I whirled around to see a perfectly formed paper airplane drifting to the floor. Then I looked up to see a pair of twinkling eyes smiling at me. I picked up the paper airplane and held it up in the light.

"Isn't this a little too energetic for a man in your condition, fly boy?"

"Had … to … get … your … attention … somehow …." Rex's voice was raspy with the oxygen hose taped to his nose.

"Yeah, I suppose you had to improvise since they took away your flash-bang devices when you checked in. Nurses hate being paged that way." I fluffed his pillow a little bit and pulled up his covers to keep him from getting chilled after his little paper airplane stunt. I wasn't going to ask how he pulled it off, given the number of tubes sticking out of him. With Rex, it's best not to ask questions. "So, how are you feeling … other than the obvious?"

"Me? … I'm … fine …. You … have … presentation … today …. SCRAM!"

As I saluted my compliance to him, Wendy came in. I turned away to give them a couple of moments of semi-privacy. She gave Rex a disapproving smirk when I showed her the paper airplane he had constructed. Then she, too, shooed me away, knowing the big presentation was in a couple of hours.

There's a point where one becomes so exhausted that sleep is elusive and delirium starts to set in. I think I was beginning to approach it as I was leaving the hospital, so I made sure to stop at the gift shop and pick up a Diet Mountain Dew and a Red Bull Tallboy. It wasn't exactly the most pleasant-tasting combination of drinks I've had, but the caffeine rush began to kick in a few minutes later, enabling me to locate my car and start driving. I called Molly to let her know Rex had regained consciousness and I was headed to the office. She wished me luck on the presentation, telling me she had heard what happened the prior day.

"Do what you have to do, Toby," she assured me. "We'll be OK regardless of what happens. If I can't get a fellowship, I can always delay the doctoral program."

Her words empowered me. Ignoring Rex's advice about guarding my inputs, I topped off my caffeine high with a stop at the Starbucks drive-through. If my calculations were correct, the buzz would end about an hour or two after the presentation. Then I could clear out the rest of my desk if it came to that, after which

I would go home and sleep it off. A quick shower and clothing change and I was meeting my team for last minute preparations right on time.

Elena must have briefed the team about Rex's incident, because I was showered with concern the moment I walked in the door. Given it was her husband who had ended up shooting and killing the criminal during the drug bust, Elena also didn't look very well rested.

"I'm alright … REALLY!" I think I was saying it more for my benefit than theirs. We ran through our slide presentation one last time, reviewing all of the flow charts and data and rationale. I didn't have the heart to tell the team it probably wouldn't matter. Rona was most likely already in Doug's office, spin-doctoring all of the reasons why I should be fired and the rest of the team should be reprimanded.

We arrived in the executive conference room and set up about a half hour before anybody else got there. As the clock on the wall approached 9:30, Doug and the board of directors began to filter in. But there was no sign of Rona. Doug had his administrative assistant run to her office while he tried to call her on both her cell phone and her home phone. There was no answer either place. He just shrugged and said something must have come up.

"We need to get on with the presentation. Toby, what have you got for us?"

The team took the same approach we had done with the managers from the other departments. We began by sharing the bottom line impacts to SysteMuscle. Then we provided some of our systems thinking techniques to demonstrate how we had arrived at our conclusions. We justified our need to expand the scope into Finance and Inventory. Both managers had shown up at our invitation, and both were passionate to share their buy-in for our solutions.

Doug began shaking his head at one point, and we thought we were in trouble. "Who put in place these policies you're trying to reverse? I don't remember ever authorizing these kinds of roadblocks in the processes."

"Rona Povo required many of them, sir," answered Elena. The managers from Finance and Inventory agreed, leaving Doug to scribble some notes in his planner, still shaking his head.

At the end of the meeting, there were head-nods all around as the other executives and board members saw the benefits of pursuing our recommendations. Doug apologized again for Rona's absence and also verbalized his approval for proceeding. He promised he would assign a project manager to work with us to make sure things were executed as presented.

I still was uneasy about Rona's absence. I figured today would still be my last day at SysteMuscle once Rona showed up and talked with Doug. I went back to my desk and fired up my laptop to read through the messages I had missed since my hasty departure the day before. Before I could get to my e-mail, a headline on the Breaking Local News section of my browser caught my eye: "Local Executive Arrested After Routine Traffic Stop."

I clicked on the link to be faced with a fresh mug shot of Rona Povo, looking highly disheveled. The story read as follows:

If you're going to speed in the West Metro, just suck it up and take your ticket and nobody gets hurt. Evidently, Rona Povo, VP of Operations for SysteMuscle, the local sporting goods distributor, missed that memo.

Povo was stopped by Sgt. Byron Torbin a little before 7 AM this morning for speeding. He clocked her going 85 MPH in a 30 MPH zone. Ms. Povo began arguing with Sgt. Torbin when he approached the car. When the verbal confrontation didn't appear to be working, Povo then got out of her car and attempted to engage Sgt. Torbin with physical intimidation. He gave her one warning to get back in the car, and she complied. And took off.

After a chase which lasted for more than a mile, Sgt. Torbin again pulled over Povo's car, although this time it was for an arrest rather than a speeding citation. While the list is still pending, Povo can expect to face multiple charges.

A record check showed Ms. Povo has an extensive history of traffic violations, and this was not her first confrontational traffic stop. A court date is pending, but sources confirmed Povo was still at the courthouse awaiting bail. Sgt. Torbin could not be reached for further comment, but is expected to be present for the court appearance with the tape of the incident recorded from his patrol car.

I called Bic immediately, not expecting him to answer given he was probably asleep and also trying to avoid calls from reporters. Surprisingly, he answered right away.

"Toby! How did your presentation go?" He bellowed before I could even say hello.

"It went great, thanks to you," I replied.

"Huh?"

"Do you remember my telling you about the difficult executive I was dealing with at my job?"

"Yeah."

"That was your arrest victim this morning."

"Rona Povo is your boss?!?! No way! Ya know, Toby, the whole time I'm running records on her, I kept thinking the name sounded familiar. Given her extensive traffic record, I figured I'd just heard about her in a briefing before, but … with everything going with Rex, it totally slipped my mind you worked for SysteMuscle. I was way too wired after we got Rex to the hospital so I went ahead and worked my scheduled shift, even though the

Captain told me not to." Bic was rambling now, obviously from the same level of fatigue impacting me.

"Well, you saved me a lot of headache by doing what you did."

"Man, if I'd've known she was your boss from hell, I'd have roughed her up a little more during the arrest," Bic laughed at his own joke. "That's one mean-spirited vixen you got there, dude."

"Based on the news story, I don't think she's going to be my boss much longer. I doubt Doug will keep her on the payroll."

"Oh no, buddy, her system is gonna have one nasty feedback loop. I'll see to it." Bic again guffawed at his own reference to systems thinking. "I gotta warn ya, though, I just heard from the station that she finally posted bail a few minutes ago. She was mad as a hornet and muttered somethin' about needin' to get to the office." His comment gave me an idea, and I quickly hit the print key for the news article.

"Hey, any news on Rex?" I asked. "I'm going to head to the hospital before I go home and crash a little later. I'm exhausted."

"Yeah, I talked to Wendy, and she said he's already been up and out of bed. The ICU nurses got sick of him real quick and sent him to a regular room. He should be settled in by now."

"Anything you want me to tell him, Bic?"

"Yeah, tell him thanks for saddlin' me with all of the paperwork from last night's bust."

"Will do. Thanks again for keeping the streets cleared."

"No problem. Stay safe, bro!" It meant a lot to me that Bic and some of his colleagues now used the terms, bro or brother, with me. I knew it was a special term for them, and not one taken lightly. Cops are a close-knit group who don't take to outsiders easily. There was no higher compliment I could receive.

As tired as I was, I had one more issue to resolve. If Rona had just been released on bail, as Bic had indicated, she'd be arriving at any minute to finish up the discussion we started yesterday. I wanted to be ready. I placed a phone call to Doug's executive assistant, asking if I could swing by to get Doug's signatures on the approval forms from the morning's presentation. If all worked as I thought it might, this could be the perfect application of pulling the trigger only when I'm ready to shoot.

I picked up the presentation binder and slipped the printed news story about Rona's arrest at the back of the packet. As I was approaching Doug's office, Rona almost ran right into me. At least her timing was perfect, if nothing else. She was not looking at all her normally groomed professional self. She stopped dead in her tracks when she saw me.

"You!" she almost screamed. Then it lowered to an audibly prolonged hiss. "You …"

"Yes, me," I responded nonchalantly, as though yesterday's conversation never occurred. "Do you have something to say, or was this exchange simply a new form of greeting? By the way, we missed you at the presentation this morning. It went very well." I decided it was best not to comment on her appearance. Some things are best kept to an inside voice.

She paused and stuttered. The anger was welling up inside of her. I tried to suppress a smile.

"I trust you'll have your boxes packed and your desk cleared out by the end of the day," she attempted a smug smirk, but given her appearance, it came across looking quite ridiculous.

"Maybe … maybe not," I countered. "I was just taking this packet of materials to Doug's office for his signature to allow the team to move forward." I lowered my voice so only she could hear it. "I wanted to resign in person to Doug. My resignation is the last page of the binder."

This news seemed to cheer Rona, and she grabbed the binder from my hands and walked right into Doug's office. I followed at a distance.

"Where the hell were you this morning? What happened to you?" Doug appeared unamused by Rona's earlier absence and present appearance when she walked into his office unannounced.

"I'm so sorry, Doug," she gushed. "I simply had the worst morning imaginable. I'll explain it to you later. I wanted to close the loop on the team's presentation this morning with your signatures, and I think there's something at the end of the packet you should see for yourself."

Doug opened the binder and flipped to the last page. Instead of finding my resignation, he found the printed article on Rona's traffic arrest. He blanched.

"Toby, would you please excuse Rona and me?" Doug asked as Rona looked smugly down her nose at me.

"Sure, Doug, my work here is done," I grinned and winked at Rona, and for the first time since I'd met her, I was able to be genuinely pleasant. "It's been interesting working with you." Her facial expression showed she had no clue what she had just prompted Doug to read. I figured he'd have found out soon enough; I merely sped up the inevitable and probably saved my own job in the process.

As Bic had indicated, Rex already looked considerably better when I went to visit him over the lunch hour. You'd think a bullet to the lung and major surgery would keep anyone in bed for days. I guess people need to know it takes a lot to keep us Donovan boys down.

"How did the presentation go?" Rex asked, the strength returning to his voice and his energy level much higher as he sat up in bed. "I heard about Bic's run-in with your boss. Who knew 'protect and serve' would go to such lengths?"

"I don't think it had much to do with protect and serve," I responded. "You've been right all along about this systems thinking stuff … on many levels. Certain things are just meant to happen in a certain way. You can't trick the feedback loop forever. Rona's inputs eventually led to her disastrous outcome. Your efforts with me and my team led to the inevitable accomplishment. In both cases, inputs drove outputs. If those things hadn't happened today, they eventually would have. That's just what occurs when you have Systems Working All Together."

Epilogue

"The only limit to our realization of tomorrow will be our doubts of today."

-Franklin Delano Roosevelt

"So what next?" Elena's question was legitimate, given that our team now had to take our suggestions and make them happen for real.

"I assume we're moving from design to action," I responded to her. Evan, Seth, and Rachel just looked bored. "What gives? We sunk a lot of effort into designing these solutions, and you've all been behind me all the way. Why the sudden round of disinterest?"

Now it was their turn to shrug at me. We'd had a few weeks off from the project while everybody dealt with the issue of Rona's hasty departure from the company. I decided to be aggressive and let Doug know my interest and ability to replace her was more than sufficient, so I was now settled into my role as VP of Operations. As the dust settled from the other organizational changes, I called this meeting so the team could refocus their energy on implementing the changes we'd designed. Unfortunately, energy was the last thing I was feeling.

"Doesn't it all seem ... well ... just kind of obvious?" asked Rachel. "I mean, we know what we need to do. Why do we need to make it into a big production with a project plan and an official kick-off and all?" In pure Rachel fashion, she managed to overdramatize the 'big production' aspect.

"Is that how the rest of you feel?" I ventured.

"Sort of," Evan offered. "We want to see these things happen. We stuck together through all of the pain of figuring out systems thinking and figuring out why our systems were broken ..."

"But ...?" I knew there had to be a 'but' in there somewhere.

"But if we know what we need to do, why do we need to create some kind of formal project to do it? Isn't project management just creating more work?" Seth's completion of Evan's thought surprised me, since Seth was the last one I'd have expected to take issue with any kind of formalized process.

"So, do you think the project stuff is overkill?" I wasn't really upset with them. I just wanted to be sure I understood where they were coming from. The question was met with emphatic nods from Rachel and Evan. Seth was less enthusiastic. Elena said nothing.

"Hmm," I mused. "It seems we're at a bit of an impasse here."

"No we're not. You know we'll do the 'good little soldier' thing and follow the rules," Rachel retorted.

"But you should know by now I'm not going to play that game. We're a team, and after all we've been through to this point, we sink or swim together."

"Fair enough," she replied. "What next?"

"Let's do a little brainstorming," I stood up and walked over to the flip chart. "What are your reservations about turning our recommendations into a formal project?"

Surprisingly, the brainstorming session was short-lived, as their concerns all centered around one key question: Why do we need a formal process to define tasks when we already know the solution? Even Seth, who could talk a great game on about any methodology, really couldn't come up with anything specific about project management to argue why it shouldn't be used. I pulled out our presentation from a few weeks prior.

"It hasn't changed," I deadpanned to their inquisitive looks. "And neither have we. So how do we get from our current state to our desired state?"

All four looked a little befuddled. A different tactic was needed.

"Elena, can you tell me just one thing we need to DO to make these recommendations happen?

"Sure, we have to build some kind of computer interface between the Call Center and the Accounting department to give us current up-to-date customer information." I smiled and wrote it on a clean flip chart.

"Give me something else," I gestured toward Seth.

"Same thing as Elena said, except for Inventory," was his response. Again, it was captured on the flip chart.

And we took every item we'd struggled with over the past few months and made a list of every action we'd need to take to get from our current state to our desired future state. We even started breaking the big tasks down into smaller tasks. By the end of our meeting, we were even able to sequence some of them.

"But aren't we getting away from the whole concept of systems thinking and SWAT?" Seth asked when he saw all of the tasks we identified.

"Not really. We've just added a new dimension to it," the words popped out almost from pure intuition. "We're just looking at the system from a new angle, from a broader view." I walked over to the whiteboard and drew the now familiar systems model with new labels:

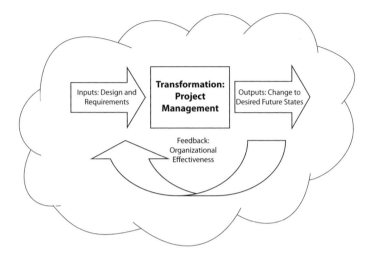

Inputs: Design and Requirements → Transformation: **Project Management** → Outputs: Change to Desired Future States

Feedback: Organizational Effectiveness

"So the tasks of the project are how we convert our inputs— our designs and requirements—into the outputs," summarized Elena.

"And the outputs are making those changes a permanent part of the company," added Seth.

"So it would seem," I was glad they were catching on quickly. "What we're ultimately after here, folks, is an accomplishment. Systems thinking helped us design our accomplishment. Office politics almost derailed our accomplishment. And project management will help us achieve our accomplishment."

"So in our case," Evan jumped in, "we knew to make our Call Center work more efficiently we needed to have a web ordering solution, which included an online catalog for both customers and dealers alike to access. We also found out we needed to improve our interfaces with the Finance and the Inventory team. Those solutions now have to be designed and planned in order to be realized."

"And those project deliverables—those outputs—become the final step in our accomplishment," Rachel rounded out the chorus of understanding.

"So, let's get on it," I challenged the team. Together, we devised a project plan, and we decided as a group that Elena would be the best fit for project manager, since she was the more technically savvy member. She had also been assigned as my backfill, now that I was taking over Rona's position, so the project manager role was a natural fit for her.

Since we all knew the tasks at hand fairly well, we decided to lay out a high level business case before jumping into formal project planning. We knew from other projects at SysteMuscle that the projects which performed the best had been thoroughly planned early in the process. As the timeline began to stretch into the following spring, Elena suggested we try to wrap up the project by mid-April.

"Well, we'll try to get it done as soon as we can, Elena, but the deadline is more dependent on how much work there is to complete rather than an arbitrary completion date," I countered, a little concerned the new project manager was adding schedule constraints before the project was even planned.

"Oh I know," Elena justified, "it's just that I'm creating another important deliverable who will be arriving sometime next April." She patted her tummy to emphasize the point.

"You mean … you're going … are you…?" I hadn't been this bad at finishing a sentence in weeks. Rachel hugged her colleague while Evan and Seth did high fives.

"Yes, fatigue and morning sickness aside, I'll be accomplishing an output of my very own in about six months," Elena explained as the meeting ended and the others filed out the door. Being the last two out, as we usually were, she changed the subject from her own health. "How is Rex doing? Tadd hasn't brought him up recently, and we've both been too distracted with other things. Besides, Tadd was more than a little shaken up after the shooting, but he's been doing much better since he's back on the force after his administrative leave."

"Rex is Rex. Solid as a rock, and ornerier than ever. I am anxious to hear how his first day back went today. The doctors wanted him off for another month, but I think it's better for his health to return early. Wendy was about to kill him. He doesn't do 'caged animal' very well."

"Well, you go on," she waved me off. "We'll get this project off the ground."

"Thanks, and congratulations again!"

I tried to pop into Doug's office to give him an update on Operations' most strategic project, but as usual he wasn't there. I packed up my stuff and headed to the car. It was great to have my own office again. Still, the new position had its challenges. Doug was as distracted as ever. He hates dealing with details as much as he loathes conflict. Unfortunately, the details and conflict surrounding Rona's departure almost put him over the edge. I was finding it difficult to get his attention and even harder to keep him focused once I got it. He still practiced his own brand of hit-and-run management, but at least I was now in a position to deal with it more effectively.

After work, I headed off to meet Rex. He was already seated in our normal booth, looking right at home in his uniform. His energy level was improving, although today he was somewhat subdued. It appeared as though he had something on his mind.

"How was the first day back? You don't look any the worse for wear, old man," I teased.

"Watch it, pup. I can still arrest you. The first day back was good. The Captain ordered me to take it easy the first couple of weeks, though."

"Good. At least somebody is making sure you behave."

Rex laughed at the thought of anybody telling him what to do. His laughter was hearty but still restrained, and I could tell there was still some pain in his side. Before I could comment on it, he changed the subject.

"So what's next for you at SysteMuscle with your favorite felon out of the way?"

I told him about my experience with the project team earlier in the day. "I thought they had come so far, but there are days they seem to be so naïve."

Rex then shared with me how Tadd had been very similar when he had first come on the force. "He was just like a puppy that was all tongue, ears, and paws. He was falling all over himself every day, and I was exhausted from chewing him out on a daily basis. But look how he turned out. I wouldn't be here today if he hadn't reacted so quickly that night in the barn. Sometimes young, impulsive, and clueless can work to your advantage. Those can be great inputs to build a really wonderful resource."

"But how did you get him to the turning point?"

"I knew what output I wanted from him, and I communicated it to him. Human behavior operates under the same principles as other systems. When he behaved in ways getting him closer to those outputs, I praised him. When he didn't, I said nothing. If he really screwed up, we talked until he could find the solution. It didn't take long for him to figure out the formula for himself. There are some people who aren't very bright, and if you find yourself fixing their inputs and coaching them with no change in behavior, then do yourself and them a favor and remove them from the system. Otherwise, they'll bring down the other people in your system."

We then talked through the issue of turning our current systems into a project. I told him how I'd surprised myself with the new dimension of systems thinking applied to project management. He just laughed as I wrapped up the recap.

"What's so funny?"

"Seems synchronicity is nipping at our heels," he replied to my puzzled look. "My team just learned the same lesson last weekend. We were practicing at one of the major corporate complexes. Talk about adding another dimension! I thought Mack Marinaro was going to jump down some throats. Our normally well-oiled machine was acting like they'd never been in a tactical situation before. We were dealing with reflections from windows and glass, visibility over cubicle walls, the sound vibrating on the floors as they walked up the halls. Finally, Mack had to remind them they were operating in a 360-degree environment."

I looked at him inquisitively.

"Most of our tactical training is fairly linear, as you've seen for yourself. We may have a two story house, but we have walls and doors and windows, and we are trained to take our stack from one end of a stronghold to the other. This was our first experience dealing with a stronghold this complex, and it was a great learning experience for the team. Our systems thinking was broadened because of the new environment and all of the other systems introduced. Mack reminded us to think in terms of things we wouldn't otherwise notice. Just because we can't see outside of our current system, doesn't mean things can't see us."

"But you're the one who taught me about SWAT. Isn't this just another example of it?"

"In a way, yes, but you have to remember the systems we discussed were fairly linear also. One system ended, and its outputs were picked up by another system. In this case, we had multiple systems all working simultaneously. It was like the systems themselves were now inputs and outputs. It's the same with your team. They thought creating the solution was enough. But all of the tasks needed to implement the solution were just lurking around the corner, and they had to broaden their horizons. Project management is just another system interacting with your design requirements. But projects are going on all around you all the time, so the design of your solution has to fit into the project environment."

"Makes sense," I acknowledged, but Rex picked up on something else in my tone.

"OK, what is it?" he barked.

"What's what?"

"Don't play this game with me. Something is bothering you."

"Alright, already. The problem is Doug."

"There's an understatement."

"I know, I know. Doug can be challenging, but I'm more concerned about getting the executives to understand systems thinking. Our most senior managers think they only need to be concerned with strategy, and they ignore all of the operations stuff until it's too late. Then they delegate or outsource their concerns to people who don't get the vision. Take Rona for instance. I think Doug might have fired her even if she hadn't been arrested by Bic that morning. When he found out she'd been putting up roadblocks to prevent us from being successful, he was pretty livid."

"Why don't you think the executives pay attention to systems thinking?" Rex inquired.

"Well, in Doug's case, I'd call it executive laziness. He would rather spend time on his recreational diversions than lead an organization. Most people I know say their executives are just too busy dealing with too much stuff. They're always reacting."

"OK, sounds fair. So they have too many inputs coming into their brains in order to focus on the really important things: setting strategy and vision and ensuring it's being carried out. Tell me if this looks accurate." Rex pulled out his notebook and flipped to an open page:

"Yeah, I guess so. But how can I help Doug leverage SWAT to make a difference in SysteMuscle?"

"Well, has Doug defined a mission or strategy for your company?"

"A few years ago. It's pretty out of date."

"This would be the first area to help him then. Encourage him to revisit the strategy."

"Could possibly be a good start, but Doug views missions and strategies as fluffy things which don't add value to the bottom line. He's a little cynical about them."

"Well, if Doug wants to continue making money himself, he'd better consider what direction he wants his company to move."

"OK, vision aside, what else can I do to help my executives achieve SWAT?"

"How are you doing with the feedback loops? Are you helping Doug spend his time on what matters?"

"Well, up until last month it wasn't an issue since Rona was always in the way. I've watched what other senior managers and company executives do, though. Some of them tend to come to him with trivial problems they should be able to solve themselves."

"So the feedback loops show he's not allowed to focus on results. He's getting pulled into his environment rather than attending to the planned outputs. No wonder he's always escaping to go play."

"I suppose you're right, Rex. But that brings me back to my earlier question. What can I do to make him successful?"

"You don't have Rona in the way any more. Have you actually talked to Doug?"

"I guess not," I conceded. "It's been a little crazy with the transition from Rona to me. And also it's been challenging getting my responsibilities transitioned to my subordinates. And now there's the project."

"Well, as you've learned about systems, if you don't take control, they'll just continue to react to you. Let Elena handle the project. Your job is to sponsor and champion it, not to manage it. You've set the vision for the project, and Elena will make sure it executes successfully. She'll also handle your former day-to-day distractions keeping you from meeting your Operations goals and mission. This frees you up to start paying attention to the critical results. And some of those results include making Doug successful."

"OK, you win. You know, did you ever consider moving from law enforcement to business?"

"Haven't you been paying attention the past few months? Law enforcement is business. When you're in law enforcement, it's all about results. We don't have a choice. And we don't always get to enjoy the results we want. Do you know how many active drug dealers in the West Metro are out on the streets because something in the system broke down? But we keep trying. We keep analyzing. We keep planning. And we keep improving. That's the heart of systems thinking." Rex was showing his passion for his profession.

"I surrender!" I chuckled with my hands up in the air. "So what all have you been up to since you've been on leave, other than having time to coach me?"

"Well, it seems we all got distracted for a while, but I wanted to share this with you," Rex pulled something out of his pocket. "The combined SWAT team decided they wanted a common patch for our uniforms. We've all been wearing subdued versions of our respective cities' police patches. But when we're on the combined SWAT team, we're all one team and we need to identify ourselves as one team."

The patch was round, about three inches in diameter and was created with subdued black and gray colors. Across the top was the word SWAT. In the center was a tactical shield super-imposed on the systems model. Along the bottom were the words, "CARPE FACTUM."

"Carpe Factum? Latin?" I asked.

"Very good. It means 'Seize the Accomplishment,'" Rex

responded. "I looked it up on the internet. Almost every other SWAT team has some kind of Latin phrase on their logo, but I wanted something a little different. As we've discussed, accomplishment is the output that counts. We all just want to accomplish something significant. For you, it's making and distributing sporting goods. For us, it's securing a stronghold and making the city a safer place to live. We each need to define our important outputs—our critical accomplishments—and seize them. So, what do you think?"

I could only think of one response appropriate for this explanation. "Dominate, dude. Dominate."

CHARACTER MAP	
Rex	Some people understand that systems thinking can be applied in any profession and any setting.
Toby	Learning to apply systems thinking universally is a key skill, and the right teachers are always there whether we know it or not.
Doug	Executives often do not like to be bothered by the systems that run their organizations ... often this can lead to disastrous results.
Rona	Setting up roadblocks in a system is dangerous when the motive is protecting one's own turf.
Elena	The quiet ones in meetings often are those with the most to share, if they can be motivated to speak up.
Rachel	The passive-aggressive resistor in meetings is great at sabotaging morale and agendas.
Evan	Some people are just resistant to change. If you can woo them away from the status quo, you can make progress.
Seth	Focuses more on tools and process than looking at the big picture of how systems work. Fads don't work; systems do.
Bic	Knowing the behavior of the system components and applying them is critical to understanding the system.
Tadd	Sometimes impetuous is a good thing to the systems model; it means knowing how to take action quickly.
Aly	Seeing beyond your own system to the relationship of multiple systems is the heart of SWAT.
Molly	Make sure that in your pursuit of your own systems goals, you are not inadvertently hindering another person from reaching theirs.

Glossary of Basic System Terms

Inputs – anything that is going into a system. It could be human, financial, material, or informational. These are the raw building blocks for creating your outputs.

Outputs – the accomplishments of your system. If your actual accomplishments are not equaling your planned accomplishments, then the outputs are out of alignment.

Transformation – the process of converting inputs to outputs. It could be a physical change, an addition, or simply a pass through the system.

Feedback – the measurements which tell you if your outputs are in alignment with the plan. The feedback loop will indicate if your inputs and/or your transformation need to change.

Environment – the playing field for your particular system(s). Generally, the environment is made up of other systems which are outside your control. If you can figure out the inputs, outputs, and feedback loop of those systems, it can become a lot easier to control the variables affecting your system(s).

Synergy – a well-operating system will create an output that is more valuable than the "sum of its parts." You see this especially in people-oriented systems that value the diversity of inputs. All of the inputs together create something that all of them acting individually never could have created.

Suboptimization – the opposite of synergy. This happens when a system never should have been created or when it needs corrective action. The inputs would have been more productive left on their own rather than having been put through the system.

Throughput – how much is actually passing through your system at once. The relationship of converting inputs to outputs.

Capacity – how much can potentially pass through your system to create usable outputs; maximum throughput.

Constraint – the smallest capacity of any part of your system. The area which creates the most bottlenecks.

Partition – categorizing a system based on various factors (large vs. small; complex vs. simple).

System Dependence – one system is impacted by another system in one direction only. System A's output is System B's input.

System Interdependence – two systems impact each other in a symbiotic relationship. System A and B each provide each other with inputs and outputs.

Delays – lapses in time within the system. This can make cause-and-effect difficult to observe when the feedback loop isn't immediate.

Entropy – the measured disorder or chaos of a system; where systems break down and become disorganized or conversely draw energy from the outside to become more orderly and organized.

Atrophy – decrease or wasting of a system because of damage or disuse.

exhibit **C**

Analyzing Your System

What kind of system are you analyzing? Is it manufacturing?
Process? Operational? Behavioral? Training?

Define the start and end of the system:

Start of system: What triggers the inputs to enter the system? When does the system "begin"?	
End of system: How do you know when the system ends? What is the output being produced?	

Define your outputs:

What are you producing? Is it tangible? Is it measurable? Is it trackable? Is it stable or dynamic?	
Does your output align with the mission or purpose of your organization? Are you truly focusing on your outputs?	

Define your inputs:

What are the inputs that are creating your outputs? From where do they come? How much control do you have over the source?	
How do your inputs work together? Are they dependent on each other when they enter the system?	
What is the timing of the inputs? Are they arriving when needed and in the correct quantities? If not, why not?	
How does your environment impact the inputs? Do they (or their characteristics and behaviors) change over time?	

160

Define your transformation:

How are your inputs converted into outputs? Are there inputs that actually distract the transformation? How?	
Are there unnecessary review steps that could be eliminated if the process were just "done right" the first time? How long do the reviews take?	
How does each step in the transformation either change the "item" being processed or add value to it in some way? Is the value defined in terms of the customer?	
What tools are available to help you with transformation? Can you map the process of transformation?	

Define your feedback:

How will you measure your output?	
How can you quantify the accomplishment? Yes/No? Number scale? Outsider input?	
Who is in charge of collecting feedback?	
What tools are available to How will interpretation of the feedback be handled? Who are the decision-makers who impact changes to the system?	
What thresholds or triggers will decide if a change is warranted?	

Define your environment:

What elements are outside of your control that impact your inputs, transformation, outputs, or feedback?	
How does your system impact its environment? Is it a positive impact or negative impact?	

Define SWAT:

What other systems' outputs serve as inputs to your system? Can you impact or change those outputs to fit your system?	
What inputs to other systems do your outputs serve? How can you communicate with those other systems to serve them better?	

Mapping Out Your Process

Flowcharting does not have to be a frightening experience. With a little practice, anybody can break down a process into its individual steps and graphically represent it so others can easily understand what is occurring. As mentioned in Chapter 3, the BRANDO steps for creating a basic deployment flowchart (or swim-lane diagram) include:

1. Boundaries: Identify where each process starts and stops.

2. Roles: Identify the general categories of responsibility rather than specific individuals for each process.

3. Activity: Identify the individual steps in the process—each action goes in a rectangle and each decision point goes in a diamond.

4. Negotiate: Review the steps for accuracy, clarity and validation.

5. Draw: Connect all of the lines among the activities and decisions; pull the process together.

6. Opportunities: Identify and discuss areas for possible improvement of the system for more effective accomplishment.

1. Boundaries: Identify where each process starts and stops.
This actually can be the most challenging step of the entire process because it can be very subjective. A little trick I learned early in my career helps me determine the starting and stopping points. For the stopping point, what is the output, outcome, or deliverable that is being produced? Are you creating the prototype for the latest and greatest widget on the market? Great! The end of the process is when you have a completed widget prototype in

hand. The start of the process may be when somebody decides that the widget prototype is necessary. This is sometimes called a "trigger event," indicating that something decides when to initiate the process.

If your process seems too large and complex, consider breaking it down into more manageable sub-processes. On the widget example, you may be creating a widget prototype, but the sub-processes may include the creation and approval of designs, the selection of materials, the set-up of the plant and machinery (or the outsourcing), etc. There are no hard and fast rules, but if you find yourself overwhelmed with the size and complexity of the process, break it down into smaller sub-processes and look for a starting and stopping point you can easily document and chart out.

> NOTE: The starting or stopping points may change as you begin flowcharting, which is acceptable. Systems and processes tend to evolve over time; why shouldn't the documentation representing them also change?

2. Roles: Identify general categories of responsibility.
This, too, may evolve over the course of documenting what is going on; however, most of us have a good idea of who is involved in creating our final output. The question you need to ask at this stage is who is touching your process. My preference is to list them in the order they are first introduced to the process.

Also, try to stick with actual roles instead of naming individual names. While Suzy, Fred, and Tom may be the only three people in the office today, it may not be the case in a month if business explodes and additional resources are brought in. Also, if multiple people fill the same role, identifying roles in a process can facilitate the creation, maintenance, and tracking of job descriptions, as well as assist in documenting performance reviews.

Widget Creation	
Project Manager	
Engineer	
Marketer	

3. Activity: Identify the individual steps in the process.

Each step in the process is important. While something may be trivial to you, it might be relevant to another person; therefore, capturing each step as it occurs can make or break your process flow. Remember that at first, you are only "roughing it out," so don't put in the lines until you have finalized your process and everybody involved substantially agrees.

Also, there are numerous software tools on the market which make flowcharting very easy. While it can be documented in PowerPoint or Word, I've found that Microsoft's Visio software is among the most effective and easiest to use. Regardless of the software tool (if any) you use, the shapes you employ to build your process should be the same.

Oval	Process terminators – denote the start and end of a process only. Generally, a process has a single starting point but may have multiple ending points.
Rectangle	Process Step – each step in the process should get its own rectangle. Do not try to put too much information in each one. Label each step beginning with an action verb.
Diamond	Decision – generally best for yes/no or other binary questions where there are only two answers. If multiple paths from the decision diamond, consider breaking it into smaller processes. For each path from the decision diamond, label the conditions (yes/no, true/false, OK/not OK) and if available, the percentage of time each path is taken.

Circle	On-Page Connector – allows for connecting two points of the process found on the same page without having to draw confusing lines intersecting other lines or boxes.
Pentagon	Off-Page Connector – allows for connecting two points of the process found on different pages; allows the process to be segmented across multiple pages.
Others	For documents, computer systems, data, input screens, etc., you may use the custom designed shapes on the software or something more intuitive.

It should also be noted that you can build deployment flowcharts either horizontally (left to right) or vertically (top to bottom), whichever you prefer. There are many who prefer one specific way of creating processes; however, if you are taking the time to document your process workflows, it already puts you light years ahead of many others, so the format and technique for me falls into the "consistent where critical, variable where valued" school of thought.

Widget Creation

As you are working through the process, if you would like to add notes or other supplemental information, you can easily enter additional documentation at the bottom of your flowchart. While building the flowchart, try to work as a team. The more people you have observing and contributing during creation (while more time consuming up front), the fewer revisions you should need to make on the back end.

It might also be useful to do a "mock run" of the process, so

166

your team can discuss it as they observe each step of the process. I've also found it useful to put yourself in the position of the "thing" being processed (e.g., customer order) to look at the process from a different angle. This also allows you to note any prolonged "down times" in the system.

4. Negotiate: Discuss for clarity, accuracy, and validation.
Before you publish the flowchart as "the way things are," it helps to have as many eyes on it as possible. As you read in the SWAT story, certain people may disagree on the way things are done. If they are major enough, discuss why the variances exist. There may be valid reasons why people perform tasks differently (or in a different sequence).

Systems should be observable, so do not fall into the trap of the "black box" where some miracle occurs and then you pick up the process again.

If people are reluctant to tell you how they do their work, it opens up a possible dialogue with them about making things better. They may be territorial about their processes, afraid they will lose power if they share. They may also be reluctant to change, fearing documentation of their current processes will mandate major changes later.

Include a sheet for approval signatures. One thing I've observed is people providing a verbal approval in one meeting only to discredit the process flow in another meeting. Ensuring the key stakeholders have signed off on the flow heightens the accountability for everyone to get it right the first time.

5. Draw: Connect the activities to pull the process together.
Very simply, this step completes the "as is" (current state) by adding any remaining details and drawing the lines among the boxes. I wait until the end to draw the lines as one addition in the middle of a process may create an unpleasant domino effect further down. By waiting to draw the lines, you can avoid a lot of rework during the editing. (*See chart on following page.*)

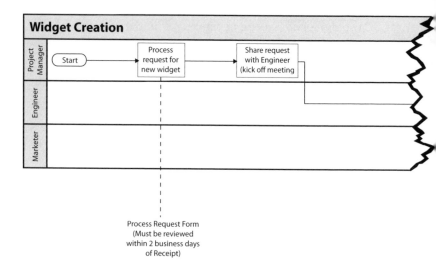

Widget Creation

Project Manager	Start → Process request for new widget → Share request with Engineer (kick off meeting
Engineer	
Marketer	

Process Request Form
(Must be reviewed
within 2 business days
of Receipt)

6. Opportunities: Discuss areas for possible improvement.
The final step is to look for opportunities to improve the
current state. This is the point where the hunt for paradigms
and "organizational sacred cows" occurs. People can be a little
defensive about the "way we've always done things" and it can
be challenging to shift their thinking to new methods and
techniques.

The first two areas for improvement I look for are lane
changes (hand-offs) and decision diamonds. Whenever you hand
off work from one person to another, there is the potential for
miscommunication or mishandling. It's like playing the game of
Telephone, where a message is whispered around a circle. What
started out as "Ted and Joan are going to see *Hercules* at the
movies" winds up as "Ron is moving foam to Hackensack." Each
hand-off represents an opportunity to streamline the process by

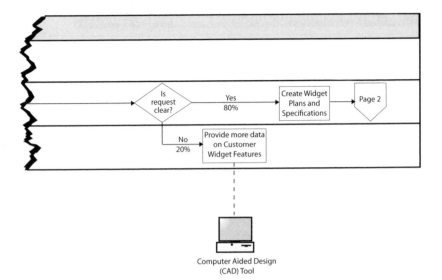

Computer Aided Design
(CAD) Tool

keeping it in the hands of one role, person, or party for as long as possible.

In the same way, each decision diamond shows that there may be multiple paths for accomplishing the same thing. From our example above, unclear requests mean a third party must be brought in to help clarify and then the process loops back to another meeting between the project manager and the engineer. While it only happens 20% of the time, what are the kinds of miscommunications that prevent the project manager from providing clear request information the first time around? These are the tough questions to ask.

Systems Thinking and Meeting Management

Every meeting is a system. You may not think of it as such but when you consider how much time is wasted in unnecessary and fruitless meetings, applying the systems thinking concepts can be very useful. After all, think about how much time you spend in meetings. Go over your schedule from the prior week and count up the number of hours you spent in meetings. Now assess how many of those meetings actually added value to your outputs or how many of those meetings to which you added value (i.e., you were the input). In brief, how many meetings led to a significant accomplishment? Pretty sobering thought, isn't it?

Very early in my career, I was given the opportunity to facilitate a quality circle. It was a positively eye opening experience to facilitate a team like that. Over the years, I've learned a lot about what helps meetings go well and what can make them go terribly wrong. My interest in systems thinking only solidified my interest in effective meeting management, as I saw many of the parallels. When you look at a meeting as a system, it becomes easier to assess how and where meetings can improve in both effectiveness and efficiency:

INPUTS

The inputs to a good meeting should be intuitive. First, determine what type of meeting you want to hold; in other words, tell people what the output will be. Is this a meeting to share information, to provide status, or to solve a problem? If the only purpose for holding a meeting is because it's 9:00 on Thursday morning, that's not a good reason.

Next, set up the agenda to align with the outputs of the meeting. Your agenda is the road map for the system. It should be defined in terms of the outputs you desire, not in terms of who wants to speak. Whose knowledge can help you arrive at the desired outputs? Are they on the attendee list? Are they scheduled to speak? What do you need them to say or do in the meeting? How much time are you giving them? What about other attendees? Will they benefit from what is in the meeting? How will you handle "uninvited guests"? Meetings quickly can be derailed by people who weren't invited and who do not add value. Are there any pre-meeting assignments? What do you want your attendees to know or do before they come into the room? Make sure the agenda is published far enough in advance to set others' expectations.

What kinds of supplies and logistics need to be considered? Where is the meeting being held? Is the room big enough? Is it set up in a way that will help you meet your desired outputs? I've seen great meetings go awry because the room was set up in a classroom style when the participants should have been facing each other. What supplies do you need? Projector? Laptop? Flip chart? Markers? Are you providing food and beverages? Is the food being catered? What kind of lead time do you need?

TRANSFORMATION

Once your agenda is published, use it to stay on track during the meeting. Tools such as Edward deBono's Six Thinking Hats® is an excellent tool to help people, but even without such techniques, simply following the agenda and staying focused on the outputs will help tremendously.

If you have a team who will be meeting repetitively over numerous weeks or months (as the team in our book did), creating a "code of conduct" (a behavioral contract) can help you mitigate some poor manners and actions. Besides the obvious (respect each other, contribute, listen, be on time), you might also have policies governing use of cell phones and PDAs. Allow people to govern and guide others' behaviors. Having a code of conduct does no good if there is no feedback loop (with consequences) for bad behavior.

Speaking of bad behavior, how do you handle those chronically dysfunctional individuals who seem to plague meetings? Their motives may vary from the innocent social faux pas to out-and-out sabotage, but they're still preventing you and your meeting from seizing your desired accomplishments. Here are some of the more common behaviors. If you try the strategies for fixing these problems and the behaviors continue, remember that you don't have to continue to invite those folks.

Behavioral Inputs	Root Causes	Fixing
Detouring: Goes off on tangents, introduces new topics with alarming frequency, takes you away from the agenda whenever possible	Need to be heard; desire to sabotage the process; need for social outlets	❑ Focus person detouring (and others) back to the agenda (and reinforce the need to follow the agenda) ❑ Use a "parking lot" (*please see page 173 for explanation*) ❑ Provide them with offline feedback about their behavior ❑ For brainstorming and idea generation, use more written than vocal techniques to express
Challenging: Will argue with anything and anybody; strong desire to be right rather than do right	Need to be right; insecurity; need to prove oneself	❑ Clarify and validate their concerns to determine how real they are ❑ Ask others if they share the same concerns or questions ❑ Provide them with offline feedback about their behavior ❑ Use more written ways of communicating rather than vocal
Distracting: Plays with laptop or PDA during meetings, takes cell calls regularly	Need to multi-task; apathy; lack of courtesy or social common sense	❑ Add rules about use of electronics to the code of conduct ❑ Have a "penalty jar" for people who violate those rules ❑ Provide them with offline feedback about their behavior ❑ Have an "exceptions clause" which must be stated at the beginning of the meeting (e.g., "I'm leaving my cell phone on because my wife is going into labor any day.")

Behavioral Inputs	Root Causes	Fixing
Monopolizing: Like to hear themselves talk, will grandstand and filibuster and just keep yapping as long as you let them	Need for attention; insecurity	▫ Take turns around the table or direct the conversation (i.e., call on specific people to contribute) ▫ Make the monopolizer be the meeting scribe (it's hard to talk and take notes at the same time) ▫ Remind them of the code of conduct ▫ Provide them with offline feedback about their behavior
Resisting: "But we've always done it this way" is this person's mantra. Any threat to the status quo is taken as a personal challenge. They don't like change	Fear of change; power of status quo; need for consistency	▫ Clarify the resistor's concerns about the change ▫ Quantify the need for change ("in the battle between drama and data, data almost always wins") ▫ Brainstorm for the positives about the change ▫ Discuss the pain points of the status quo ▫ Ask for additional research (if needed)
Do-Nothing: This is the person who is physically present in the meeting but says nothing	Fear of speaking up or failure; apathy; inability to interrupt	▫ Determine if the problem is one of apathy, shyness, passive-aggression, or some other reason ▫ Call on the silence-type directly ▫ Affirm the value the silence-type brings to the meeting; remind them of past victories ▫ Provide them with offline feedback about their behavior ▫ Level the playing field if others in the meeting are more outspoken
Non-showing: This is the person who is invited but never shows up	Schedule conflicts; apathy; inability to see value; priority issues	▫ Validate the reason for the no-show. Are the meetings consistently being held at bad times? Are you providing enough lead time to schedule? ▫ Ask the person if they could send a "proxy" to take their place in the meetings. ▫ Work with the person to see if other things can be removed from their schedule/responsibilities to get them to the meetings

NOTE: A parking lot is a means of capturing any extra information not pertinent to the agenda. It may be an irrelevant tangent or a valid issue that needs to be addressed. Usually, I just keep an extra sheet of flip chart paper in the room and mark it as the "parking lot." When items come up that threaten to derail the agenda and goals, I simply write them on the parking lot. This allows the meeting to continue according to the agenda.

OUTPUTS AND FEEDBACK LOOP

Meeting minutes should be produced as a tangible artifact from every meeting. At a minimum, the minutes should tell when the meeting was held, who was in attendance (and possibly who was absent), the decisions, the issues, and the action items. The results should be objective and tangible, so that follow-through and accountability can occur.

Any action item should include the following:

- ❑ What needs to be produced

- ❑ Who is accountable for the results

- ❑ Who is responsible for working with the accountable person to ensure follow-through

- ❑ Completion date

- ❑ Any issues or assumptions affecting the action item

Ensure that people have enough heads-up to be able to follow through on their assignments. If people do not follow through as committed, document it. Let people know the number of times they didn't follow through on their commitments, and ask them for a new completion date. If you create a culture of accountability (i.e., a strong feedback loop), you will be more likely to have tasks completed.

ENVIRONMENT

Many of the same rules that apply for face-to-face meetings also apply for remote meetings (conference calls, video conferences, and webchats). Use courtesy and common sense. On conference calls and videoconferencing, make sure people know who is talking. On video especially, be aware of any personal habits that the camera may pick up (just because people are not in the room, doesn't mean they can't see you).

For webchats, be especially careful about what you say and

how you say it. People do not always have the benefit of seeing facial expressions or hearing vocal tones or interpreting body language. Also, if you are sharing your computer desktop with others in a virtual meeting setting, watch out for any instant messaging or embarrassing screen savers which could affect your message or your reputation.

With available technology, it is also possible to have more sidebar discussions than ever before. Text messaging and cell phones make it possible to hold conversations outside of the main meeting communication, so defining and holding to a code of conduct will serve you well.

Favorite Systems Thinking Resources

Systems Thinking, Systems Practice. Checkland, Peter. Wiley © 1999

Slack: Getting Past Burnout, Busywork, and the Myth of Total Efficiency. DeMarco, Tom. Broadway © 2002

Rethinking the Fifth Discipline. Flood, Robert Louis. Routledge © 1999

Outliers: The Story of Success. Gladwell, Malcolm. Little, Brown, and Company © 2008

Grow or Die: The Unifying Principle of Transformation. Land, George. CEF Press/Wiley © 1997

The Fifth Disciple – The Art and Practice of the Learning Organization. Senge, Peter. Broadway Business © 2006

An Introduction to General Systems Thinking. Weinberg, Gerald. Dorset House © 2001

Quality Software Management: Volume 1 Systems Thinking. Weinberg, Gerald. Dorset House © 1991

Unstuck: A Tool for Yourself, Your Team, and Your World. Yamashita, Keith and Sandra Spataro. Portfolio Trade © 2007

About the Author

Timothy L. Johnson is the Chief Accomplishment Officer of Carpe Factum, Inc. Two decades of experience in project management, systems thinking, business analysis, and team facilitation have culminated in a laser-focused mission to help organizations "seize the accomplishment." He is certified as a Project Management Professional (PMP®) and has held project leadership roles ranging from multi-billion dollar class action lawsuit settlements to training video production, from major software transformation to strategic design. His work on myriad projects of varying sizes for multiple organizations allows him to help organizations and individuals identify and manage the factors that help and hinder achieving the accomplishments for which they are destined. Past clients include Harley-Davidson Motorcycles, Teva Pharmaceuticals, Wells Fargo and Principal Financial Group.

Timothy is available for executive coaching, keynote speeches, and workshops. You may find out more about his services, as well as read his blog, at his website, www.carpefactum.com. Timothy is also a regular contributor to www.office-politics.com. He resides in Des Moines, Iowa with his family.